The Education Reform Act

Competition and Control

Leslie Bash and David Coulby

CASSELL

Cassell Educational Limited
Artillery House
Artillery Row
London SW1P 1RT

First published 1989

**British Library Cataloguing
in Publication Data**
Bash, Leslie
    The Education Reform Act.
    1. England. Education. Law: Education Act 1988
    I. Title   II. Coulby, David
    344.204′7

    ISBN 0–304–31768–3

Typeset in Linotype Century Schoolbook by
Fakenham Photosetting Ltd., Fakenham, Norfolk
Printed and bound in Great Britain by
Biddles Ltd., Guildford and King's Lynn

Contents

Preface

Whether or not all the terms of the 1988 Education Reform Act are ever implemented, it represents the most important governmental initiative in the education service of England and Wales since 1944. It has fundamentally and probably irreversibly transformed the nature of state education. This book seeks to explain how the Act came about, what its terms are and what its likely effects will be.

The book falls into three parts. The first two chapters outline the political and philosophical context from which the Act derived. They are in no sense a history of education in the period which preceded the Act but rather a selection of events and ideas that informed the political process. Chapters 3 to 7 look in detail at the terms of the Act and their likely effects, with chapters on the structural organization of schools, the national curriculum, the break-up of the ILEA, further education and finally higher education. The final three chapters examine in more detail some of the policy contradictions both within the Act and between the Act and other areas of social and educational policy, analysing the effects the Act will have both on children and young people and on wider society.

Although the chapters written by each of the co-authors are identified, there was considerable co-operation and mutual agreement at each stage of the writing of the book.

All commentators on the Act must be grateful to Julian Haviland, who so speedily published the responses to the consultation round—which the government would have preferred us not to see—while the Bill was still before Parliament. We are grateful to colleagues and students at Bath College of Higher Education and at Mid-Kent College for helpful discussions concerning many aspects of the Act. We are exceedingly grateful to Crispin Jones and John Raynor for discussing an earlier draft of the book with us. The death of John Raynor, while this book was being published, was a major academic loss to us, as to so many in the educational world. It would have been impossible to produce the book at an early stage without the invaluable contributions of Crispin Jones and the Bristol Polytechnic Study Group. In particular we wish to thank Jacquie Coulby and Angie Genn-Bash for advice, encouragement and forbearance (the latter, in her role as economist, was especially helpful in discussing early drafts of Chapter 2).

We wish to dedicate this book to Alexander, Emma, Isobel, William and Oliver, together with all other children whose entitlement to a high-quality state education has been jeopardized by the passing of the 1988 Education Reform Act.

1

From Educational Partnership to Central Control

David Coulby

INTRODUCTION

Whether deliberately or fortuitously, the 1944 Education Act, and the legislative arrangements made within its framework up to 1988, established a balance of control in educational institutions. When it was working successfully this balance could be referred to as a partnership. The partners were the Church and the State with regard to voluntary-aided provision and the teaching of religion in schools. Local and central democratic government each had an important part to play in a national system locally administered. Teachers and head teachers, within broad constraints, had responsibility for the curriculum, its delivery and, up to the age of 15, its assessment. Universities could control what courses they taught and, within the peer review system, so, to a lesser extent, could public sector higher education institutions. The local education authorities (LEAs), the Department of Education and Science (DES) (as it was ultimately to become) and the teachers, represented through their unions, each had areas of responsibility throughout the education system which amounted to a balance of control.

The passing of the Education Reform Act on 29 July 1988 dramatically broke this balance and shifted huge areas of control over educational institutions to the Secretary of State at the DES. The amount of central control given by the Act to the Secretary of State is unprecedented. Speaking against the Bill (introduced by his own party) at its second reading in the Commons, former Prime Minister Heath said: 'The Secretary of State has taken more powers under the Bill than any other member of the Cabinet, more than my right honourable friends the Chancellor of the Exchequer, the Secretary of State for Defence and the Secretary of State for Social Services' (quoted in Wragg, 1988, p.16).

How had confidence in teachers and LEAs been so eroded that such legislation was considered necessary? How had the professional status and established power of these two participants in

3

the partnership been weakened so that it could be so forcefully overthrown? It is these questions that this chapter seeks to answer. Later sections deal with the teachers and the LEAs. The next section provides a broader introduction that considers the notion of consensus, which is the way in which the post-1944 partnership is traditionally presented. In each section it is necessary to consider all levels of the education system. Within the constraints of space, contemporary statements and documents are considered. This is not to imply that one speech or one document could change the history of educational institutions. It is rather to provide access to the terms and arguments within which contemporary participants saw educational decisions being made.

THE CONCEPT OF CONSENSUS OVER EDUCATIONAL POLICY

A tempting assumption with regard to recent educational history in the UK is that there was a consensus between the main political parties on educational issues from the passing of the 1944 Education Act to, say, then Prime Minister Callaghan's Ruskin College speech of 1976. The evidence for such an assumption is superficially convincing. The 1944 Act, drawn up by the Conservative minister Butler, was enthusiastically implemented by the Attlee post-war Labour government. It was Labour that laid the foundations for the tripartite secondary school system with its associated eleven-plus tests. These tests in their turn tended to dominate the upper primary curriculum. Labour politicians, often themselves the products of successful grammar school education, were reluctant converts to the cause of comprehensivization. The Robbins Report of 1963 (Committee on Higher Education, 1963), with its recommendations to expand higher education to meet the demands of all those who were 'able' to follow degree-level courses, was likewise apparently acceptable to both parties. During the 1960s the power of the eleven-plus was gradually being eroded, but open conflicts seemed to remain comparatively rare. The Plowden Report (Central Advisory Council for Education, 1967) offered a widely accepted celebration of the emerging progressive curriculum and methods of English and Welsh primary schools. Similarly, compensatory education and positive discrimination were widely seen as strong tools to deal with any possible educational disadvantage.

Crucial to this illusory consensus was the uncritical acceptance by Labour politicians of the notion of 'ability'. This is one of the key terms of the 1944 Act and it remains an important justification of practice in educational institutions in the UK today. Once the

4

term is accepted, it follows that pupils can be ranked according to their putative ability or intelligence. Ranking schools according to the tripartite system or organizing groups of pupils into streams are institutional practices which can be justified by a commitment to this notion. Similarly, higher education can be made available to all those sufficiently 'intelligent' to follow the courses. Of course those without such 'intelligence' will not need higher education and will be suitably placed in the lower strata of the workforce. The effects of policies based on this belief were, perhaps, not clearly visible in the late 1940s. In the event it was working-class children who were to be seen by schools as lacking in ability, who were to end up in the secondary modern schools and the bottom streams of comprehensives. The modest expansion of higher education in the late 1960s was mainly to benefit middle-class young people. Working-class pupils, whatever their putative ability, were not finding their way in appropriate numbers into higher education (Halsey *et al*, 1980).

This is not the place to contest the notion of ability (see Bash *et al*, 1985). The point is that it and its associated institutional arrangements were the unsound foundations on which the illusion of political consensus was erected. Opposition to these institutional arrangements centred around the drive towards comprehensivization. The two main structural changes in the period 1944–1976 were perhaps comprehensivization and the consolidation of the polytechnics. Both these developments succeeded to some degree in undermining the elitist system established by the 1944 Act. Yet here again the consensus explanation would seem to persist. Conservative Leicestershire was at the forefront of comprehensivization, and the other right-wing rural areas, such as Oxfordshire and Cambridgeshire, were cited for their good practice in terms of community comprehensive education. Similarly, local education authorities of whatever political complexion were anxious to develop the status symbol of controlling a higher education institution. Despite this, on the issue of comprehensivization in particular the idea of the existence of a consensus is misleading (see Centre for Contemporary Cultural Studies, 1981) because it conceals the strong undercurrents of dissent. The voice of the *Black Papers* (Cox & Dyson, 1969) was derided at the end of the 1960s as the dying chant of defeated elitism. In the 1980s this voice was to be the dominant counsel in the formation of Draconian education policy change. The Tameside case revealed that opposition to the consensus was political as well as rhetorical.

In the mid-1970s Tameside LEA was engaged in a legal battle with the Labour-controlled DES to prevent the scheme of

5

comprehensivization that the DES was trying to introduce by means of a Circular. Tameside won its case in 1976, thereby not only revealing the illusory nature of the consensus, at least as far as it had been applied to comprehensivization, but also demonstrating that the 1944 framework did not allow the DES to control the education system by means of Circulars. Any government that wished to introduce major educational reform would need to do so through central legislation. Further, any government determined on reform would need to take account of recalcitrant LEAs. The Tameside case demonstrated that the power of the LEAs under the 1944 Act was something which would need to be reckoned with (or overthrown) by any government whose educational programme was so firmly held that they wished it to be homogeneously implemented across England and Wales. The 1944 'consensus' rested on a balance of Church and State and crucially of local and central government. As soon as any political party developed an educational policy that required universal implementation this consensus could be revealed as illusory. The proponents and opponents of comprehensivization were committed to such universalist policies. Once one of these sides consolidated central power, the extent to which local opposition could be tolerated would be severely limited.

Embedded in the notion of consensus is the acceptance that education is a professional issue and that decisions with regard to it are best taken by professionals or, at least, on the basis of their advice. As long as this belief was accepted then considerable power could rest not only with LEAs but also with head teachers and teachers. Structural arrangements within a school were thus largely at the discretion of the head teacher in consultation with the rest of the staff. Crucially, control over the school curriculum was in large degree in the control of teachers. Undeniably, there were constraints on this control, notably, at secondary level, that exerted by the examination boards. Nevertheless, as eleven-plus testing was gradually abolished, the control of the primary curriculum and that of secondary schools at least up to the end of the third year rested very largely with teachers. Teacher autonomy and the idea that politics could somehow be kept out of education was another aspect of the consensus which was to be undermined. Although this process was a gradual one, an important landmark was Callaghan's Ruskin speech of 1976.

In considering this speech it is important to emphasize that politicians were not, at least at this stage, interested in control for control's sake. The desire to take control from the professionals stemmed from a dissatisfaction with the products of the education system. Part of the background to this is the growth of unemployment, gradual but incremental in the late 1970s and rapid in the early 1980s. This unemployment was particularly prevalent among young people and particularly concentrated in urban areas. The link between youth unemployment and deficient schooling was irresistible to industrialists (Weinstock, 1976) and to politicians of both major parties. Indeed by 1976 there was almost a consensus that was critical of the state education system. The techniques of innuendo and faint praise used in the Callaghan speech were indicative of a real and general dissatisfaction with state education. Since 1976 national confidence in state schooling and in professional autonomy has by no means been restored. The criticisms made by Callaghan were to be echoed on all sides during the next decade.

> I am concerned on my journeys to find complaints from industry that new recruits from the schools sometimes do not have the basic tools to do the job that is required. I have been concerned to find that many of our best trained students who have completed the higher levels of education at university or polytechnic have no desire or intention of joining industry. Their preferences are to stay in academic life (very pleasant I know) or to find their way into the civil service. There seems to be a need for a more technological bias in science teaching that will lead towards practical applications in industry rather than towards academic studies....
>
> On another aspect there is the unease felt by parents and teachers about the new informal methods of teaching which seem to produce excellent results when they are in well qualified hands but are much more dubious in their effects when they are not. They seem to be best accepted, if I may judge from my own experience, where there are strong parent–teacher links ...
>
> It is not my intention to become enmeshed in such problems as whether there should be a basic curriculum with universal standards—although I am inclined to think that there should be....
>
> There is no virtue in producing socially well adjusted members of society who are unemployed because they do not have the skills.
>
> (Callaghan, 1976)

In this speech and in the numerous statements of which it is representative there is a fallacious and facile link between education and unemployment (Bash *et al*, 1985). Unemployment was

7

generated not by failures in the state education system but by shifts in the national and international economy. When the economy had been growing, industry had had no difficulty in providing the training it considered appropriate. No matter how well educated or well trained UK school leavers had been, the 1970s and 1980s would still have been periods of massive structural unemployment: the possible point of application for ameliorative measures would have been the economy itself, not the education system.

A 'great debate' followed the Ruskin speech, one of the outcomes of which was the formation of the Manpower Services Commission (MSC), now the Department of Employment (Training Agency). The MSC began to develop Youth Opportunities Programmes which were the precursors of the Youth Training Scheme (YTS). The MSC was established by Labour with trade union support. In the hands of the Thatcher administration which came to power in 1979, the MSC was a major vehicle for change: firstly in the further education sector; secondly via the Technical and Vocational Education Initiative (TVEI) in the curriculum of secondary schools; thirdly, via the Enterprise Programme, in the courses and teaching of higher education institutions.

Callaghan had placed the issue of school and work at the centre of the political agenda: 'There is little wrong with the range and diversity of our courses. But is there sufficient thoroughness and depth in those required in after life [*sic*] to make a living' (Callaghan, 1976). The stance adopted by the MSC and its subsequent political supporters was to carry this further. For them unemployment was seen not as the result of the decline in British industry and commerce, but as the result of unemployed young people lacking relevant skills and knowledge. Once the victims are blamed in this way, then their schooling is also open to attack. If, after 11 years of compulsory schooling, the young people still could not find jobs, then surely the schools had been wasting rather a lot of their time.

> Even now, at a time of very high unemployment, some [firms] lack key technical and professional skills, particularly in new growth sectors. There is a great risk that the ability to take advantage of an economic upturn will be severely constrained by such shortages and by the inability of firms to adapt swiftly enough.... Young people face special difficulties and youth unemployment has risen to the point where 1 in 6 of all those unemployed is under 19. Many older workers, even when they have opportunities, find the new requirements too demanding. In many parts of the country, local

communities are in decline because they lack the skills required to attract inward investment or enable new local enterprise to flourish.... Meanwhile, at school young people have often been less well prepared than they should be for working life. The vocational relevance of much that they have been taught has not been made clear to them.

(MSC, 1981, pp.2–3)

This quotation is from an MSC document of 1981, long before unemployment reached its peak, yet it reveals the way in which blame for a major national dilemma was being shifted away from the government and employers and on to schools and young people.

THE EROSION OF TEACHERS' PROFESSIONALISM

Attacks on teachers and schools became more frequent and more fierce as the 1980s progressed. Sir Keith Joseph, as long-standing Secretary of State for Education and Science, carried out a sustained attack on 'the ineffective teacher'. This was a successful populist position as it provided an easy target for parental dissatisfactions. One of its culminations was Clause 49 of the 1986 Education Act, which legislated for the regular appraisal of teachers. However, the power of the attack was wider than this, as, by implication, the whole teaching profession could be seen as idle or ineffective. It encouraged parental and public scrutiny and criticism of the work of teachers. Disruption in schools, for instance, always a popular press theme, could be blamed on 'the ineffective teacher's' failure to keep control (Coulby, 1988).

The long-running pay dispute and strikes of 1986 and 1987 further exposed teachers to criticism by parents, politicians and the media. The strikes were mainly but not exclusively about pay. They were also a result of the decline of the status of the teaching profession and its increasing removal from the process of educational policy formulation. The abolition of the Schools Council by Joseph was a clear indication that the voice of the profession was no longer to be heeded in curricular and examination policy at national level. The creation and expansion of the MSC undermined the influence of the profession as well as that of the DES and the LEAs. The movement towards educational reform, which had gathered strength around the Ruskin speech, was not led by teachers, nor was their advice sought by its perpetrators. Teachers were to be the victims rather than the agents of this wave of educational change.

One of the consequences of the strike was to leave the teachers'

9

unions divided and powerless just at a time when education was being placed at the top of the national agenda. Once the 1986/87 strikes, which were partly motivated by the perceived erosion of professional status, were underway, they left teachers vulnerable to just those stereotypes that the right-wing press and politicians were trying to attach to the profession. 'Ineffective teachers' were behaving in an unprofessional way and damaging the educational opportunities of their pupils. This was an argument that could be understood by every parent pulled away from work to look after children who were not at school because of the strikes. The strikes provided the opportunity to direct attention away from teacher shortages and dilapidated and under-resourced schools and towards the teachers and their unions. The strikes brought education into the news as a regular item in the run-up to the 1987 election. The new Secretary of State, Kenneth Baker, eager for political success and less hidebound than his predecessor, was able to end the strike and strip the teachers' unions of their negotiation rights. The teachers were defeated, discredited and demoralized, but education had become a matter of great national concern. Far from being the advocates of any developments, teachers found that their power and discretion were aspects of the system that future legislation would endeavour to curb. Callaghan had claimed—albeit reluctantly—that he did not wish to become enmeshed in the debate about 'a basic curriculum with universal standards' (Callaghan, 1976) and over a decade passed before central government acknowledged that this was precisely how they did wish to be enmeshed. By the time of the publication of the 1987 consultation document *The National Curriculum* (DES and Welsh Office, 1987), it had been decided that what was taught in the schools of England and Wales was far too important to be left to teachers.

THE BACKLASH AGAINST LOCAL EDUCATION AUTHORITIES

The wider context of the backlash against local education authorities was that of a divided nation. Although, in popular terms, this was seen as a north–south divide, at least as important was the division between the run-down inner cities and the more prosperous suburban, new town and rural hinterlands. This latter division is not simply one between rich and poor regions (although this is at the heart of it), it is also reflected at the political level. The inner cities are, in the main, the strongholds of Labour power. Sheffield, for instance, has had a Labour council for many years and has persistently pushed through socialist policies at the local level, not least with regard to education. The Labour group in control of

Liverpool council was much publicized in the run-up to the 1987 general election as it was purged by the Kinnock leadership. The policies adopted by these inner city LEAs and their place in the breakdown of the educational partnership are examined below.

The inner cities were also the sites for the most dramatic manifestations of resistance against economic decline, unemployment and the associated harsh measures of policing and control. Small-scale urban collective violence has become as regular a feature of the 1980s as the visibly abrasive policing methods with which it is associated. Football violence, Saturday night violence, New Year's Eve violence have become regular patters of street life, even in smaller centres such as Leicester and Nottingham. Mid-way through Thatcher's second elected term large-scale urban violence erupted in Handsworth, Brixton and Tottenham. The Broadwater Farm riot was of a seriousness and scale to form more than a media-generated crisis.

One of the more astonishing responses to the Broadwater Farm riot, and one voiced by the Prime Minister herself, was an attempt to deflect the responsibility on to schools. Although, on serious reflection, few could believe that the disorder of unemployed and soon-to-be unemployed young people could be laid at the door of their schooling, the education policies of inner city councils were moving into the limelight of media and central government scrutiny.

During the 1980s LEAs had, with varying degrees of success and commitment, drawn up and implemented equal opportunities policies. This was not an exclusively left-wing preoccupation. A radical lead had come from Berkshire, and although this county's policy was cautiously implemented, it provided a model for use by other LEAs, in particular by the Inner London Education Authority (ILEA). The initiating issue for many of these policies was often race: in many cases they were developments of multicultural or multi-ethnic education policies. In the case of Berkshire, for instance, headings from 'Education for Racial Equality: policy paper 3' are as follows:

> 1. To promote understanding of the principles and practices of racial equality and justice, and commitment to them. . . .
> 2. To identify and remove all practices, procedures and customs which discriminate against ethnic minority people and to replace them with procedures with [*sic*] are fair to all. . . .
> 3. To encourage ethnic minority parents and communities to be fully involved in the decision-making processes which affect the education of their children. . . . To increase the

influence of ethnic minority parents, organisations and communities by supporting educational and cultural projects which they themselves initiate.... To encourage the recruitment of ethnic minority teachers, administrators and other staff at all levels, and the appointment of ethnic minority governors....

6. To monitor and evaluate the implementation of County Council policies, and to make changes and corrections as appropriate.

(quoted in Swann, 1985, pp.376–9)

Later policies, however, gained both strength and depth by the frequent inclusion of class, gender, handicap and, latterly, sexual orientation. ILEA's 'Anti-Sexist Statement' provides an example of the pervasiveness of these elements and of the seriousness with which the aspirations of these policies were addressed. In view of the criticisms that these policies were subsequently to provoke and the role of such criticism in the breaking up of the educational partnership, it is worth quoting this document at some length to provide an example.

1. The Inner London Education Authority is committed to achieving an education service which provides equality of opportunity and freedom from discrimination on grounds of race, sex, class, sexuality or disability in both education and employment....

2. We live in a society in which the process of sex-stereotyping leads people to conform to gender roles which can inhibit individuals' abilities, preferences and aspirations. The effects of sexism impoverish both sexes by limiting horizons and restricting choices.... Despite the formal availability of equal opportunities within the ILEA, in practice girls and boys, women and men make stereotyped subject choices and apply and use their achievement for different purposes when they leave the education system.

3. Although both sexes are affected by sexism, it is girls and women who suffer most. This is because sexism does not simply encourage a neutral segregation of the sexes, but is based on and perpetuates the notion of male superiority. Greater value and status is more often given to traditionally male pursuits and occupations than to traditionally female ones....

4. Passive support for equal opportunities is not sufficient to challenge sex-stereotyping. Sexism affects everyone and tackling it must be the responsibility of all. Each sector of the

education service, including those working in single sex schools, the post-school sector, the administration, the support services and the Inspectorate must play a part. The commitment and involvement of parents and governors is also vital to the practical implementation of the policy....

5. The ILEA recognises that education is a powerful vehicle for transmitting values. It can also challenge them. The Authority firmly believes that sexism is incompatible with good educational practice in all sectors of education, and that a commitment to anti-sexism is a fundamental legal and educational duty.... All educational establishments within the Authority should be assisted in placing anti-sexism, alongside anti-racism, at the heart of educational good practice. Only in this way will *all* our pupils and students reap the full benefit of the education service we provide.

(ILEA, 1985, p.4)

A central concern of these policies is with prejudice and discrimination on whatever basis. In seeking to combat these the policies could be seen as aspects of widely accepted and long-standing national policy on sexual and racial equality. A further element within them is frequently a concern with differential achievement in schools: the fact that in various aspects of school experience black children, girls and working-class children seem to progress less rapidly than the norm. The policies thus, typically, have components concerned with racial or sexual abuse or harassment, with stereotyping, achievement, curriculum change, organizational change and with implementation via governors, head teachers, teaching and non-teaching staff.

Although equal opportunities policies were widespread across the LEAs of England and Wales they were regarded with particular importance in urban areas. This emphasis is hardly surprising as these are precisely the areas where high concentrations of working-class and black children live. Issues of prejudice and underachievement are daily experiences for teachers and administrators in the inner city. Consequently urban LEAs phrased their policies with extra clarity and directness and implemented them with appropriate urgency. Of course, these were precisely the LEAs that were Labour controlled and that, as such, were opposed to many aspects of central government policy. It was perhaps inevitable, but none the less regrettable, that equal opportunities policies were dragged into the arena of party politics. If the Labour-controlled urban LEAs were in favour of equal opportunities in education, it almost seemed as if the Conservative-controlled DES had to be against them. Of course, there were strong anti-egalitarian forces within and behind the Thatcher government, and her supporters in the press had never been enthusiastic about equal chances for blacks, working-class people or women. The opposition to equal opportunities policies in education, covert at first, gathered strength as the party boundaries became fixed.

By the mid-1980s this opposition, although initially not a central policy thrust, was beginning to make its presence felt. For instance, the Council for National Academic Awards (CNAA), the largest degree-awarding authority in the UK, came into unexpected difficulties with its 1985 discussion paper on 'Multicultural Education'. Because of the right-wing presence on the Council, and possibly political interference, this paper was never fully endorsed. The references to racism were seen as too strong and as political, but the teacher educators, from whom the paper emanated, were unwilling to water it down. The document remains as a 'discussion paper' in the CNAA portfolio. Similarly, at this time it was noted that DES administrators and HMI had become suspicious about the use of terms such as 'racist' and 'anti-racist'.

In the pre-general election period specific equal opportunities issues were taken up by the right-wing press. It is necessary to stress that this concentration was on a small area of policy of a few LEAs. The intricacies of urban education policies became front page news in first the creation of and then the attack on the 'loony left'. Since this politicization was taking place against the background of the teachers' strike, the attack had a blunderbuss effect: it could hit the left-wing, Labour-controlled LEAs and the (striking and therefore leftist, not to mention 'ineffective') teachers with one range of fire. The right-wing press developed a form of anti-anti-racism which, in the close scrutiny it gave to senior black appointments, for instance, was difficult to distinguish from racism *per se*.

It was the homosexuality issue that provided the preferred and perfect target for the rightist press and politicians. Once discrimination and prejudice against homosexuals had been accepted as an equal opportunities issue, then sexual orientation (or 'sexuality' in the quotation from ILEA above) was added as a plank to the platform. The equivalent of racism or sexism was then termed heterosexualism. But anti-heterosexualism could easily be presented by right-wing politicians and press as the encouragement of homosexuality in pupils in schools. In the run-up to the general election blatant prejudice against homosexuals became a commonplace populist theme, and this prejudice was used to give further

14

emotive force to the criticism of educational equal opportunities programmes.

The London Borough of Haringey was the particular target in this respect, but allegations were also made against other urban LEAs, particularly the ILEA. The popular parody of policies on homosexuality had the advantage of smearing all equal opportunities policies as 'loony' by connection. Attacks on tolerance for homosexuals are frequently an aspect of bigotry and persecution associated with the centralist state. In the context of equal opportunities in education such attacks can further be seen as a commentary on the gender role issue. Behind these attacks is an atavistic insistence that men should be men and women should be women. In so far as this intolerance insists on stereotypical gender roles, family patterns and divisions of labour, it forms one aspect of a fundamental attack on the freedoms and opportunities of girls and women.

Blame was now being firmly placed on LEAs as well as on teachers. The movement that culminated in the centralist Education Reform Act arose from distrust of these two key elements in the education system. The Act thus seeks to empower other constituents (parents, head teachers, governors, industrialists) over those who had traditionally seen themselves as the main providers of education. These latter were seen to be too far out of line with central government aspirations ('ineffective' and 'loony left'). These themes can be illustrated by the Prime Minister's triumphalist address to the 1987 Conservative party conference; the general election by then had been won and the new legislation was being drawn up:

> But it's the plight of individual boys and girls which worries me most. Too often, our children don't get the education they need—the education they deserve. And in the inner cities—where youngsters must have a decent education if they are to have a better future—that opportunity is all too often snatched from them by hard-left education authorities and extremist teachers. Children who need to be able to count and multiply are learning anti-racist mathematics—whatever that may be. Children who need to be able to express themselves in clear English are being taught political slogans. Children who need to be taught to respect traditional moral values are being taught that they have an inalienable right to be gay.... We are now about to take two dramatic steps forward in extending choice in education. First, we will allow popular schools to take in as many children as space will

15

permit. This will stop local authorities putting artificially low limits on entry to good schools. And second, we will give parents and governors the right to take their children's school out of the hands of the local authority.

(Thatcher, 1987)

Events in the London Borough of Brent played a key part in the development of this eschatology. The suspension of a head teacher for an alleged racist remark brought Brent on to the front pages. The formation of the Development Plan for Race Equality (DPRE), using mostly central government funds derived from the Home Office via Section 11, provided Brent with a large team of advisory teachers. These curriculum development workers were dubbed 'race spies' by the media on the totally unsubstantiated assumption that they would be visiting schools on the lookout for other teachers and heads who might make racist remarks. Secretary of State Baker sent HMI into Brent to investigate. This fire-brigade use of HMI only added to fears that they were being politicized. While HMI were in Brent, the press coverage culminated in a fiercely biased *Panorama* programme. In the event, HMI were able to demonstrate their professional autonomy. Their report clearly indicated that much of the press coverage of Brent had been misleading and alarmist.

158. In general the race and gender policies of the Authority either had no more than a modest effect on the quality of provision, or where they were more clearly apparent they had beneficial effects. In spite of considerable public agitation on these matters there was no evidence that the quality of work is being threatened or the curricula of the schools are being distorted as a result of schools applying Brent's anti-sexist and anti-racist policies, though in primary schools they may have diverted attention away from other pressing curricular issues....

160. The LEA's anti-racist policy had some beneficial effects. Possibly its principal achievement was its contribution to the racial harmony which prevailed between the pupils both in the primary and secondary schools.... The general impression is that the Authority's anti-racist policy goes with the grain of local opinion, has fairly widespread support in the schools and has a generally helpful effect on work in classrooms.

(HMI, 1987, pp. 42–3)

In the run-up to the general election the balanced findings of HMI were swept aside not only by the media but also by the Secretary of State.

Having been for so long an item of little importance on the national agenda, education was to be a central issue in the 1987 general election. The radical and confrontational stance of Secretary of State Joseph had helped to bring it to the forefront. The teachers' strikes had made education national news and a daily preoccupation for many families. Baker, a new and ambitious Secretary of State, anxious to make a claim for leadership, was determined to keep education in the public eye. In the course of the 1987 election campaign it appeared that the Prime Minister and the Secretary of State were by no means agreed about the nature of the proposed educational reform. It was the Prime Minister who insisted on the radical opting-out policies as her way of disestablishing local education authority schooling. The popular rhetoric of the day concealed the fact that the proclaimed '*denationalization*' of schools and colleges was actually a delocalization and a centralization—bluntly *nationalization*. Central government was poised to take control of schools, colleges and polytechnics away from local education authorities.

The wider philosophical justifications for the changes were those familiar from other areas of successive Thatcher government policy, notably from her management of economic affairs. These wider policies and philosophies are examined in the next chapter.

REFERENCES

- Bash, L., Coulby, D. & Jones, C. (1985) *Urban Schooling: Theory and Practice*. London: Cassell.
- Callaghan, J. (1976) Ruskin College Speech.
- Central Advisory Council for Education, England (1967) *Children and Their Primary Schools: A Report* (The Plowden Report). London: HMSO.
- Centre for Contemporary Cultural Studies (1981) *Unpopular Education: Schooling and Social Democracy in England since 1944*. London: Hutchinson.
- Committee on Higher Education (1963) *The Robbins Report* (Cmnd 2154). London: HMSO.
- Coulby, D. (1988) Classroom disruption, educational theory and the beleaguered teacher. In Slee, R. (ed.) *Discipline in Schools: A Curriculum Perspective*. Melbourne: Macmillan.
- Cox, C.B. & Dyson, A.E. (eds) (1969) *Fight for Education: A Black Paper*. London: Critical Quarterly Society.

- DES and Welsh Office (1987) *The National Curriculum 5–16: A Consultation Document*. London: DES.
- Halsey, A.H. *et al.* (1980) *Origins and Destinations*. Oxford: Oxford University Press.
- HMI (1987) *Educational Provision in the London Borough of Brent*. London: DES.
- ILEA (1985) *Race, Sex and Class 6. A Policy for Equality: Sex*. London: ILEA.
- Manpower Services Commission (1981) *A New Training Initiative: A Consultation Document*. London: DTI.
- Swann, M. (1985) *Education for All: the Report of the Committee of Inquiry into the Education of Children from Ethnic Minority Groups*. London: HMSO.
- Thatcher, M. (1987) Speech to the Conservative Party Conference.
- Weinstock, A. (1976) I blame the teachers. *Times Educational Supplement*, 23 January, p.2.
- Wragg, T. (1988) *Education in the Market Place: The Ideology behind the 1988 Education Bill*. London: National Union of Teachers.

2
Education Goes to Market

Leslie Bash

PERFECT COMPETITION

The *market* is now a dominant theme in the formulation of UK educational policy. Classical free-market economics is currently a major aspect of national politics and has been for about the past 10 years. The significance of this theory for social and economic policy in general and education policy in particular requires careful consideration. It is beyond the brief of this book to analyse free-market economic theory in any detail but without an appreciation of some of the underlying tenets it will not be possible to understand the driving force behind current educational legislation.

At its simplest, the image is that of a medieval-type market with numerous stall-holders. Each stall-holder is selling a service—education—that is pretty much the same as the service provided by each of the others. That is to say, educational resources, human and otherwise, are more or less evenly distributed throughout the market. Potential customers are free to enter and leave the market, to buy or not to buy as they wish. Assuming that demand is fairly evenly spread throughout the buying public then it is probable that each of the stall-holders will make a living and the customers will generally be satisfied. As a result, there is what is called a perfectly competitive market operating to the benefit of all without any need for state intervention.

Understandably, the reader might regard this as an idealistic fantasy. Indeed, perfect competition has long been regarded by most economists as simply a theoretical construct (Burke *et al*, 1988, p.52). However, it must be said that it has strong ideological force, which influences the course of economic argument in general and, currently, of educational argument in particular. It is important, then, to examine the concept of the free market as applied to education and to consider the immense difficulties associated with attempts to make it work. The conditions necessary for the existence of a free market may be set out:

1. There are many buyers and sellers.

2. Buyers and sellers have perfect knowledge of market events.
3. The product or service is the same everywhere.
4. Buyers and sellers operate independently.
5. Sellers are free to enter or leave production and are able to supply whatever is needed to meet demand.

(Ritson, cited in Burke *et al*, 1988, p.52)

It is worth unpacking each of these conditions to try to assess their relevance to the supply of and demand for education. The first condition, that there should be many sellers (providers), is a central tenet of the free-market approach to education. Hitherto, it is contended, the provision of public education has been a monopolistic enterprise, carved up regionally between different local education authorities and their attendant bureaucracies. This system is now superseded, even though the new legislation leaves considerable controlling power in the hands of the Secretary of State. It might be entertaining to ask if there is to be a move from a situation of monopolistic supply to one of state franchise, rather like 'independent' petrol stations or public houses which, in reality, are subordinated to the oil companies or brewers that supply them. To put it another way, will schools, particularly those that have opted out of local authority control (see Chapter 3) in the newly formed market, be little more than the hamburger joints or instant print shops of the educational world? If that is indeed the case it surely supports the increasing cynicism regarding the way in which competition will work in practice.

At the same time, it is evident that the number of buyers of education is considerable (although somewhat distorted as a result of the compulsory character of schooling). Perhaps a preliminary question needs to be posed: who exactly are the buyers? The government view is that they are not those who are the direct consumers of education, the children, but rather their parents. This appears to be based on the assumption that parents are owners of their offspring, which in itself raises further questions regarding children as property.

This question is of some importance particularly if the second condition for a free market is examined. From the buyers' standpoint, it is the children rather than the parents who will tend to have knowledge of market events. Only they will have direct knowledge of the educational product, especially if they have attended more than one school at a particular level; only they are likely to possess enough knowledge of the service to know whether to buy or not to buy. Indeed, the incidence of truancy may, in part, bear witness to this fact. But if parents are the customers, they

20

might gain direct knowledge through participation in the activities of schools (for example, sitting in classes and wandering in playgrounds). It is more likely that schools will provide the necessary information through advertising and public relations (as they are required to by the 1986 Education Act). Even so, it may not be possible to gain real knowledge of the educational service on offer without having spent some considerable time consuming it. In practice, knowledge will be based on a mixture of written information, school PR (such as meetings with head teachers or open days) and hearsay.

Given the third condition, that the educational product should be the same everywhere (which is embedded in the idea of a national core curriculum), why should the consumer prefer school A to school B? The answer is that a school is much more than what is contained in the timetable. Schools are children-processing institutions: they offer the opportunity to instil an appropriate set of values, to prepare children for life outside and to provide them with a status in society. Different schools, therefore, have different traditions and different reputations. It might be concluded, in a somewhat crude fashion, that consumer choice would be in the packaging of the product rather than the product itself. However, this would not be entirely fair since for many the packaging is just as important, indeed a fundamental part of the entire schooling process. Parents are concerned for their children's happiness at school, they worry about their behaviour; in short, they want their kids to go to what may be commonly accepted as a good school.

On the supply side, the question of how much knowledge the producers (i.e. the local education authorities and the teachers) have of education raises some interesting issues. Do LEAs know what is going on in their schools and in the education world at large? Is there loyalty to the product which actually prevents a cool appraisal of it? The answers to these questions suggest a tremendous variability regarding knowledge of the educational service on offer in particular educational institutions. Teachers very often are unaware of what neighbouring schools do, and, what is more, may not regard this as having any significance either for their own practice or for a broader knowledge of educational processes.

The fourth condition of a free market, that buyers and sellers should operate independently, makes sense in relation to education if it is accepted that the product is purely for personal consumption or investment purposes. It would be improper, as well as negating free-market principles, if schools formed cartels to fix fees or carved up the market. Likewise, if parents combined to

21

force schools to lower their fees it would restrict competition among the providers.

Finally, the fifth condition suggests that anyone who wants to establish a school can do so, and, presumably, anyone who wishes to teach may work in a school. If that is so, then whatever the demand for education the supply will in the long run be able to meet it. This point is particularly important as far as the 1988 Act is concerned. The loosening of the ties between local education authorities and schools, through the devolution of budgetary powers and the establishment of grant-maintained institutions, is supposed to help promote competition among schools. As the Education Secretary has stated, there should be greater rivalry among schools to encourage teachers towards a more competitive and less cloistered world (*The Guardian*, 28 July 1988). The major difficulty with this line of thinking is that freedom to enter or leave the market is supposed to apply to consumers too. The notion of compulsory schooling is directly antithetical to the theory of the free market. If parents are to be free to choose they should, at least in theory, be free to choose not to have their children educated at school at all.

NOT QUITE PERFECT COMPETITION

If the idea of perfect competition in education is as naive as in any other context, then the *monopolistic* competition model (Chamberlain, cited in Burke *et al*, 1988, pp. 54–5) may be more acceptable. Here, the service offered is similar in character but not identical. Schools will (as most have tended to do) offer broadly similar curricular packages (encouraged by the national curriculum) but will offer marginal differences—the type that parents can easily latch on to (as indicated previously). But instead of parents being restricted in their choice of school they will now be able to choose from a wide number of homogeneous products differentiated by such marginal differences.

THE FREE MARKET AND POLITICAL IDEOLOGY

The belief that consumers should have choice has underpinned key aspects of the current educational legislation. The capacity to choose implies that people have a degree of control over their lives. Classical economics as a constituent of nineteenth-century liberalism dwelt upon this as a major determining factor in the stability of the nation. That is to say, national stability was seen to arise from each individual pursuing his or her own ends. The result was a balanced society since not everyone would want the same thing; scarcity was unproblematic since it would be sorted out by the price mechanism. While the 1988 Education Act fails to establish a pure market system for the production and consumption of educational services it does suggest that educational stability will arise as a consequence of parents exercising differential choice. In other words, the pursuit of self-interest is, in the long run, of benefit to all.

Interestingly, not all classical liberal thinkers considered that the free market was able to deal with every human need. John Stuart Mill, writing in 1833, was at pains to point to the dangers of parental choice in an unfettered educational market:

> We may ask, whether ... the plan of nineteen-twentieths of our unendowed schools, be not an organized system of charlatanerie for imposing upon the ignorance of parents? Whether parents do, in point of fact, prove themselves as solicitous, and as well qualified, to judge rightly of the merits of places of education, as the theory of Adam Smith supposes? ... Whether the necessity of keeping parents in good humour does not too often, instead of rendering the education better, render it worse ... ?

> (Mill, 1833, pp.24–5)

Mill's reference to endowed schools foreshadowed the emergence of a publicly maintained system in which teachers and representatives of the community would have a significant amount of control over the content and structure of education. The Thatcherite view, however, is that entrenched bureaucracies and sectional interests have prevented the emergence of educational stability and an appropriate social hierarchy. It suggests that education has suffered in the post-war years from excessive local authority control. This is regarded as the legacy of municipal socialism with its emphasis on the need for a planned society, for universal health care and social security, and for greater equality between social classes.

A major difficulty for the Thatcher government was the 1944 Education Act. While it preserved some of the many cherished traditions of English education (including a strong religious element) and, indeed, maintained a spirit of competition through an emphasis on diversity of provision according to 'age, ability and aptitude', it also provided the framework for local authority dominion. Certainly, the powers of local education authorities were consolidated and some even pushed ahead with the introduction of comprehensive schools, notably the former London County Council (with its 1947 plan for partial secondary reorganization) and Anglesey, which completely reorganized along comprehensive lines in 1953 (Lawson & Silver, 1973, pp.423–4). Many would argue that this reorganization was at the expense of parents who viewed the tripartite system as providing the best means for educational, social and economic advance.

The new Conservatism, which may be dated from 1975 (Thatcher's rise to the leadership position), demanded a break with state planning (both central and local) as a means of achieving politically desirable goals. Indeed, such goals were not actually to be seen as political but rather as the province of individuals. The defence of the realm and the maintenance of social order were certainly political goals and, as such, must be provided for by the state, but the same could not necessarily be said of housing, health or education. The idea that the state has a responsibility to engineer the structure of society in order to achieve more equality is one that, according to free-market ideology, must be questioned. Not only is the collectivist philosophy of socialism challenged but also the more limited interventionism of Keynes and Beveridge. For now, the market is not only seen as a way of describing economic activity under capitalism, it is positively invoked by writers such as Friedrich Hayek (1944) and Milton Friedman (1962) as the basis of the good society.

THE FREE MARKET AND EDUCATIONAL IDEOLOGY

It is important to consider some of these ideas within the context of education. A basic tenet of the type of free-market philosophy associated with Hayek is that state intervention in people's lives is likely to result in the tyranny of a fascist or communist dictatorship; but individuals should be free to control their own lives. The prevalance of the entrepreneurial spirit in society should ensure the dynamism of an economic system based upon individual freedom. Thus, not only should the education system be freed from the shackles of state socialist ideology to become responsive to individual consumers, it should also be proactive in the promotion of values and attitudes relevant to an advanced capitalist economy.

Accordingly, entrepreneurialism must become a fundamental aspect of education, especially at the secondary and post-compulsory levels. The Austrian school of economists emphasizes the importance of entrepreneurial alertness in contributing to growth in the economy. It is necessary to allow individuals, as both consumers and producers, the freedom to be creative in their actions (see Burke *et al*, 1988, pp.66–71). In education this means that parents and employers should be enabled to make their preferences known to the producers, prompting innovation in the schools and colleges. At the same time, schools and colleges have the responsibility of promoting such individualism among students; this is seen as an essential element of socialization into a free society.

Where entrepreneurialism is interpreted in terms of the release of creativity and the contribution of innovative ideas and action to the furtherance of educational and social objectives there can be little argument. However, under capitalism the entrepreneurial spirit is rather more closely linked with the profit motive and the general making of money. Thus, the successful entrepreneur is one who reckons that if:

> you see a firm dominating the potato crisp market, you search for new types of savoury snacks. . . . You make square-shaped crisps, or ones shaped like space monsters.

> (Burke *et al*, 1988, p.69)

Likewise, an essentially similar educational product can be sold through different glossy brochures to give the impression of wide consumer choice.

We are brought to the conclusion that the free-market approach to education locks it into a set of beliefs concerning the way in which society should operate, especially with regard to its economic structure. Further and higher education have a clear function: the provision of courses that will directly contribute to economic development in relation both to individual firms and to the nation as a whole. Indeed, the current view is that colleges, polytechnics and universities should be subject to the laws of supply and demand and thus enjoined to meet the rapidly changing requirements of commerce and industry. Equally, schools have two distinct preparatory functions: the inculcation of appropriate attitudes to economic life, and acquaintance with the skills and knowledge required for the world of work. There should therefore be a smooth transition of people from school to post-school, whether in further or higher education, in a training scheme, in employment or as consumers of goods and services.

At the same time, the market approach continues to exert quite a different influence upon the course of educational policy. Here, the international market for goods and services is invoked to support policies which tend towards some degree of centralization. The perceived threat of commercial competition from other countries provides the impetus for the establishment of a set of national educational standards against which the attainment of children might be judged. The idea of a national curriculum is generally linked with official anxiety about the economic success of other countries. As the DES consultative document stated:

> We must raise standards consistently, and at least as quickly as they are in competitor countries.
>
> (DES and Welsh Office, 1987, p.3)

This is seen as a consequence of the readiness of foreign governments to impose a set of national curricular aims and objectives upon their schools. In other words successful education practices and systems are those that breed successful economies in the international market.

The educational system of the Federal German Republic is constantly cited as a major factor in its achievement of a post-war economic miracle. In particular, the vocational education (dual apprenticeship) system of the FRG is held up as the model of successful work training and one to be emulated by the UK. Although Japan's education system is not given the same high profile (especially since there is a very high staying-on rate at school), the competitive character of Japanese education is not seen to be unrelated to its legendary economic success. In fact, there are numerous examples of national education systems where a centrally imposed uniform curriculum prevails. The conclusion must surely be that the UK's failure to compete in the international market is in large measure a function of an education system that allows individual local education authorities and, in practice, individual head teachers to decide on the content of the curriculum. The result is a variably educated population with only a patchy understanding of the new technological basis of manufacture and commerce.

There is, of course, a fundamental difficulty with this kind of argument. If it is accepted that educational systems are historical outcomes of complex social, political and economic processes then the crude borrowing of such systems by governments of other countries carries certain dangers. First, it assumes that it is possible to isolate education as the key factor in relation to social, political or economic outcomes. Secondly, it assumes that it is technically feasible to undertake this activity without changing the essential features of the borrowed system. Consequently, it has been strongly argued that the Youth Training Scheme has turned out to be a distortion of the FRG's dual apprenticeship system (which, incidentally, had been criticized for being too narrowly craft-based and not future-oriented). This is largely because, unlike in the FGR, in Britain there has been little centralized direction of the school–work transition process (Noah & Eckstein, 1988, p.64). The new structures created by government, based upon the Manpower Services Commission, were hurriedly put into place, with little heed paid to the general context of educational development.

A more serious criticism of the proposal to establish a national curriculum is that it calls into question the place of the free market. Is the national curriculum to be seen as no more than a necessary regulatory framework (in Hayek's terms) for effective competition to take place? This is doubtful, for such a framework would have nothing to say about the nature of the product or service; it would simply ensure that there were no barriers to entry to the market and that conditions were set for effective competition. At this stage, it should be noted that fee-paying schools and city technology colleges are not to be constrained in this manner. Thus, competition will be between local authority/grant-maintained national curriculum schools and fee-paying schools. However, as noted earlier, it is likely that parents will come to accept this degree of uniformity and view the market in terms of what else schools have to offer.

If the place of free-market ideology in education is now established it is quite another thing to see it operating in practice. Many would contend that while the state is in a position to manipulate both the supply of and the demand for education the chances of a free market existing at all are very close to zero. The current legislation concentrates more power to control the market into the hands of central government than ever before. No school can change its fundamental mode of operation unless the Secretary of State agrees and, despite the proposal to devolve financial management to individual educational institutions, it is doubtful if these institutions would ever be allowed to raise capital in the commercial money markets (as ordinary businesses do). While further and higher education institutions are likely to become ever more tied to the world of business for financial support, schools, because of their somewhat different function, will, it seems, have to rely upon public money. It may be that there will be a few city technology colleges sponsored by industry and that voluntary schools will continue to be aided by the various religious bodies, but this will represent only a tiny proportion of total school funding.

This is by no means the whole story. The significance of the free-market concept in education may not lie primarily in its economic validity. Indeed, there are few who believe that it can work in anything like its pure form. Even the proponents of the voucher

27

system must concede that the free market is violated simply because parents would have to spend their (tax funded) vouchers in a particular manner, i.e. on schooling; they would not be free to choose to spend them on health care, on foreign holidays or in betting shops! Nowhere is it suggested that parents have the right *not* to have their children educated, in the same way that they have the right not to buy hamburgers from McDonalds. On the contrary, it is because there is a recognition that there is some universal right to be educated (and that in the past this right was not always available in practice because of the fee-paying basis of schools) that compulsory schooling was established. The only exception is the continuing right for parents, if suitable arrangements can be made, to educate their children at home.

More to the point is the extent to which the market approach has become part of conventional educational wisdom. Traditionally, philosophers and religious teachers have been among the most influential of educational theorists; in more recent times psychologists and sociologists have come to dominate. Respectively, the nature of human beings, their moral behaviour, their intellectual development and their social origins and destinies have been the preoccupations of theorists and practitioners influenced by these different disciplines. For all that, it emerges that what is considered to be an appropriate way of organizing education in terms of both its form and its content rests upon a set of ideas and beliefs ultimately rooted in the structure of society. In short, it is impossible to escape from the conclusion that educational theory is grounded in ideology.

It would appear that there is a clear ideology associated with the free-market approach to education. It is one that views education as disconnected from fundamental aspects of social relations: in short, education is *commodified*. As a commodity, education is to be bought and sold in response to rationally based demand, whether originating from parents or from employers. Education is no longer to be seen as a reflection of the collective wishes and hopes of society. It is now much more explicitly associated with sectional interests that manifest themselves in the context of the market. Parents, given increased choice, are even more likely to use other parents of a perceived similar social status as a reference point for their decision on which school is best. It is only in a situation where choice is more limited and schooling is largely determined by geographical factors that there is some chance that parents will remain oriented to what is perceived to be the local community.

EDUCATION, THE MARKET AND THE CULT OF INDIVIDUALISM

One of the fundamental attractions of the free market lies in the promotion of the individual and the demotion of the group. A market approach to life avoids the need to become involved in complex social relationships. The dominant relationship is contractual: it is characterized by rational calculation of costs and benefits. Accordingly, education is seen as personal consumption or investment, to be purchased like any other commodity or service that may be marketed. This is not to say that the personal consumption/investment view of education is entirely a product of Thatcherite culture. There would be very few parents who did not have some regard for qualifications or job prospects in respect of their offspring. But now, this appears to have become the dominant value, eclipsing any idea that parents may have educational concerns in common.

The atomization of society is very much part of the new Conservatism along with the de-legitimation of the collectivity as a unit of action. The market operates on the basis of individualism, so hindering collective action either on the part of parents (as members of a local authority defined community) or on the part of teachers (as members of trade unions seeking to impose uniform conditions of pay and service). The market reinforces conservative behaviour patterns and promotes individuals and their families at the expense of broader social groupings. Moreover, the market is bound to promote education as a positional good (Hirsch, 1977, pp. 48–51), where, because it conveys information about the individual who possesses it relative to those who do not, it also encourages individuals continually to want to move ahead of the pack. It does not matter, therefore, that through collective political action the amount and quality of education available to everyone might have improved in significant measure, since this would not satisfy those who see education as the key to elite positions. It is easy to see, then, that goods such as education 'tend to be bid up as they become scarcer in relation to the rising effective demand' (Hirsch, 1977, p.27).

This is defended, since many have said that individual parents have all too often been forgotten in the continual battles between local education authorities, teachers and central government over educational policy and teachers' pay. Yet despite government protestations that education has for too long been under the control of what it terms the producers, there is little evidence from the operation of the market elsewhere that power will in future reside with the consumers. Given what was stated at the

beginning of this chapter, there can be little doubt that the idea of a
perfectly competitive market is something of a fiction: the domina-
tion of the market by a few large producers is frequently the case,
whether in the market for detergents or for newspapers. Consumers may well find that in practice the educational market will
offer as much choice as Henry Ford offered in colours of motor cars.
Perhaps this is neatly summed up in the view that 'while the right
wishes for a free market in goods, it is increasingly and even more
stridently demanding a monopoly in ideas' (Straw, 1987, p.18). It is
the task of the remaining chapters of this book to show how the
ideology of the free market, together with the rest of government
policy, has fared in relation to specific aspects of the new legislative framework.

REFERENCES

• Burke, T., Genn-Bash, A. & Haines, B. (1988) *Competition in Theory and Practice*. London: Croom Helm.
• DES and Welsh Office (1987) *The National Curriculum 5–16: A Consultation Document*. London: HMSO.
• Friedman, M. (1962) *Capitalism and Freedom*. Chicago/London: University of Chicago Press.
• Hayek, F.A. (1944) *The Road to Serfdom*. London: Routledge.
• Hirsch, F. (1977) *Social Limits to Growth*. London: Routledge.
• Lawson, J. & Silver, H. (1973) *A Social History of Educationn in England*. London: Methuen.
• Mill, J.S. (1833) The right and wrong of state interference with corporation and church property. In *Dissertations and Discussions*. London: Routledge.
• Noah, H.J. & Eckstein, M.A. (1988) Business and industry involvement with education in Britain, France and Germany. In Lauglo, J. & Lillis, K. (eds), *Vocationalizing Education*. Oxford: Pergamon.
• Straw, J. (1987) The evasions of a window cleaner. *New Statesman*, 23 October.

3
Restructuring the Education System?

Bristol Polytechnic Education Study Group
(Nick Clough, Veronica Lee, Ian Menter,
Tony Trodd and Geoff Whitty)

The government claims to be 'taking action to increase the autonomy of schools and their responsiveness to parental wishes' (DES, 1987a). The proposals on open enrolment, financial delegation, grant-maintained schools and City Technology Colleges are all regarded by the government as consistent with this aim. They are presented by the Government as building upon the parental choice provisions of the 1980 Education Act and, more particularly, those of the 1986 Education (No. 2) Act, which enhanced the powers of governors, increased the influence on governing bodies of parents and members of the local business community and required LEAs to publish details of the costs incurred by particular schools. Yet, potentially, these aspects of the Act could make a significant contribution to a radical restructuring of the whole education system far beyond anything envisaged when the first Thatcher government came to power in 1979. In this chapter we describe and critically examine those structural elements in the Education Reform Act that affect schools and seek to understand how they relate to each other and to other aspects of current policy. In so doing, we also look at the changing position of teachers within the system and consider questions relating to special educational needs in order to illustrate some of our concerns about the impact of the Act. Finally, we point to some of the possible long-term implications of the changes.

OPEN ENROLMENT

The open enrolment provisions of the Education Reform Act require LEAs to abandon the planned admission levels (PALs) of Section 15 of the 1980 Education Act. Under that system, within the context of falling rolls in secondary schools, the LEAs could determine the limits to admission for their schools together with the criteria for admission in the case of oversubscription. Since a purpose of this legislation was to balance parental choice against the need for LEAs to maintain a viable number of pupils in each of

31

their secondary schools or to plan school closures in a manner that took into account the needs of the authority as a whole, PALs could be set significantly below a school's physical capacity. The setting of PALs up to 20 per cent below a school's 'standard number' (effectively its capacity as defined by enrolments in 1979/80) did not require reference to the Secretary of State and even lower numbers could be set with DES approval.

The implications of this approach are well summarized by a few key sentences in a letter from the Director of Education in Avon in July 1988 to parents who were not offered their first choice of secondary school:

> Under Section 6 of the Education Act 1980, which governs the matter of parental choice, the local education authority is not bound to comply with the wishes of parents when such compliance would prejudice the provision of efficient education or the efficient use of resources.... Admission arrangements ... take account of the effect of one school upon another.... The admission of a child to a school over and above the relevant PAL for the school concerned when a place is available within the PAL at an alternative school would be prejudicial to the overall planning and provision of efficient education within the context of an efficient use of resources

Now the government's rhetoric on 'parental choice', which was but one element of the 1980 Act, has been given virtually free rein in the thinking behind Sections 26–32 of the Education Reform Act. In the associated consultative document, the practice of applying PALs, which is based on a notion of the common good, is described as a process by which 'artificial limits are placed on the ability of popular schools to recruit up to their available capacity' and which has 'inhibited and delayed the necessary rationalisation of schools and at the same time acted as a barrier to the exercise of effective parental choice' (DES, 1987b). The government has legislated to provide for any school to admit pupils right up to its 'standard number' if the level of applications warrants it. Even though rolls were relatively high in 1979, popular schools with the requisite physical space can be permitted to take a higher number, but LEAs will only be able to lower the 'standard number' of a school through referral to the Secretary of State. Physical capacity is the only valid criterion for such an application, although the legislation also provides for the protection of the character of selective schools. Effectively, the role of LEAs in planning the size and number of schools in an area will be replaced by system in which this is determined through the 'market' of parental choice.

Although, at this stage, it is only possible to estimate what the likely effects of this legislation will be, many commentators fear that popular schools will become either larger or more selective in their intakes, leaving the others (and the children in them) to their fate. In general terms, the loss of pupils to the 'popular' schools will clearly have a damaging effect on other schools, both in terms of resources (especially in the context of local financial management) and in terms of morale. It is likely to encourage the re-introduction of covert selective admission to those 'popular' schools, which would further erode the comprehensive ideal and the principles of education for all. All this is apparently in the cause of increasing parental choice, which LEAs claim is already met in 95 per cent of cases. Furthermore, the open market orientation of the proposals could exacerbate divisions that already exist in society by favouring those with the cultural resources to make informed choices, and creating a stratum of 'sink' schools where pupils will have less than equal opportunity unless LEAs are able to intervene to ensure that they have adequate resources.

A case study written in November 1987 by Howard Fielding, then acting Chief Education Officer for Somerset, highlights both the disruption and the expense that could result from the policy of open enrolment. Basing his study on a town in Somerset where there are three comprehensive schools, he emphasizes the success of the use of PALs over the past three years.

> Over the 3 years, 1621 out of 1701 children have gone to the school of their parents' first choice, that is 95% immediately granted their first choice. Of the 80 parents refused over the 3 years, only 27 have appealed and 21 of these were successful. So, at the end of the process required under the present legislation, only 6 out of 1701, or 0.3% have finally been forced to an unacceptable school. In 1987, this figure was absolutely nil. Therefore, from the local authority's point of view, the use of PALs has been particularly successful. All 3 schools have been kept viable with entries above 150 a year each, and the fluctuation of popularity between schools has been ironed out.

(Fielding, 1987)

Fielding's prognosis of a likely scenario under open enrolment is that one of the schools will suffer a considerable loss of intake, forcing the authority to decide whether to prop up the school or close it. He calculates the financial implications of both courses of action. To supply the extra staff to keep the school viable would involve the employment of 18.8 teachers at a cost of £230,000 per year. It is likely that the parents of the children at the school would be less satisfied than they are currently. Closure of the school would involve providing new accommodation at the other two schools, which, after the sale of the one site, would still require at least £300,000 of capital finance, even supposing that this extra accommodation could be housed on one of the other sites. This is not in fact the reality of the situation, as to close the school would actually involve a more complex rebuilding programme at even greater cost. Fielding comments:

> Most sensible readers will believe we have reached a laughable conclusion which would never happen. But let us remember that if events do turn out this way, and it only needs one school unfairly to acquire a bad reputation, the law would require that this conclusion was reached. Would anyone feel this to be an improvement on the present situation with so many satisfied parents?

While Howard Fielding's article focuses on issues of difficulties of resource management under a policy of open enrolment, commentators from urban areas have expressed additional fears that such a policy will lead to racially segregated schools. This concern was given added weight by the occurrence of what has become known as the 'Dewsbury affair'. At the beginning of the school year in 1987, national media attention was focused on 25 children in Dewsbury whose parents had refused to enrol them at the school that they had been allocated by Kirklees Education Authority. At this school, Headfield, 85 per cent of the pupils were of Asian origin. Overthorpe, the school to which the parents wanted their children to go, was predominantly white. There was much debate about the parents' motivation and in particular whether their actions were racist. However, in making their case, the parents themselves frequently invoked 'parental choice', the right of parents to choose their children's school, which had been such a central part of the government's rhetoric about improving education (Sutcliffe, 1987).

The Labour Party has been anxious to point out the similar consequences of the open enrolment proposals especially when combined with the provisions for schools to opt out of LEA control. In the House of Commons in December 1987, their senior spokesperson, Jack Straw, said: 'These proposals will lead to educational apartheid and racially segregated schools' (quoted in Weekes, 1987). When the Bill was being debated in the House of Lords in May 1988, the opposition lost an amendment which would have allowed an education authority to reduce pupil numbers 'if they caused an undesirable imbalance in racial composition which might prejudice racial harmony within the school or the community'. Baroness Hooper, the government's education spokesperson in the Upper House at the time, argued that racial prejudice was impossible to legislate against: 'Segregation is no part of this Bill. We underline the fact that in giving parents choice, we do not wish to circumscribe that choice in any way' (Blackburne, 1988b).

FINANCIAL DELEGATION

The theme of removing decision-making from LEA members and officers, and in this case delegating it to governors and head teachers, is a feature of the new arrangements for the financial management of LEA maintained schools introduced by Sections 33–51 of the Act. Financial delegation, variously known as local financial management (LFM) or local management of schools (LMS), is seen as a way of improving the quality of teaching and learning in schools because it will:

(a) enable governing bodies and head teachers of schools to plan their use of resources to maximum effect in accordance with their own needs and priorities; and

(b) make schools more responsive to their clients—parents, pupils, the local community and employers.

(DES, 1987c)

The government is therefore seeking maximum delegation of financial and managerial power to governing bodies as is consistent with the discharge by the Secretary of State and by the LEA of their continuing statutory responsibilities. Under the terms of Section 33 of the Act, all LEAs will be required to submit to the Secretary of State schemes of financial delegation covering all county and voluntary secondary schools and primary schools with 200 or more pupils on roll. LEAs may choose to extend delegation to smaller primary schools and to special schools and the Secretary of State may require this in due course. Initial schemes for LEAs outside inner London have to be lodged with the Secretary of State by 30 September 1989, with a view to their introduction in April 1990 and their full implementation by April 1993.

The Schemes submitted to the Secretary of State will have to include:

(a) a schedule of all county and voluntary schools in the LEA, their numbers on roll and an indication of those that are to receive delegated budgets;

35

(b) the items of expenditure that will be delegated and those that will be retained under the LEA's direct control;

(c) the 'formula' for determining each school's budget share;

(d) the conditions relating to the exercise of delegated powers by the governing bodies;

(e) the arrangements and timetable for introduction of the scheme and for the training of those concerned with it; and

(f) the procedures for monitoring and evaluating the scheme, including the performance indicators that the LEA proposes to apply to its schools

(DES, 1988a)

The delegated budgets are to include staffing, books and equipment and other goods and services used by the schools (including examination fees), and day-to-day premises costs, including rent and rates. Budgets for certain other items, such as school meals and specialist services, may also be delegated at the discretion of the LEA. Capital spending and debt charges are to be excluded under Section 38(4) of the Act. Various other items will be excluded, at least for the time being, including central administration, inspection and advisory services and home to school transport, and also education support grants, LEA training grants scheme (or GRIST) allocations, Section 11 grants, travellers' children grants and TVEI funding. This does not mean that such funds cannot be disbursed to individual schools, as is the case with GRIST monies in many authorities. It means rather that they cannot be part of the delegated budget of a school in the terms of the Act. They must remain earmarked for particular purposes and cannot be redeployed by the governors in the same way as items in the core delegated budget. Nevertheless, the government's policy is to limit centrally provided services to a minimum that can be clearly justified in the interests of efficiency and effectiveness. It looks for the eventual delegation of up to 93 per cent of an authority's schools budget, although this is probably exclusive of the mandatory exemptions. In general, schemes are expected to make the real costs of as many services as possible visible to their users, while giving schools the maximum scope to carry out activities in the way that most suits their needs. Yet, as many critics have pointed out, allocating funds to schools on the basis of the average rather than real costs of items such as teachers' salaries, as initially proposed, will leave some schools with welcome surpluses while others with the same level of needs will be forced into making cuts (Muffett, 1988).

The crucial issue in all this, of course, is the formula that will be used by LEAs to delegate budgets to schools. Although this can vary from LEA to LEA, the government has issued guidance in terms of which the Secretary of State will decide whether to approve, modify or impose an alternative for any proposed scheme. It is intended that, once the 'aggregated schools budget' has been determined by approved means, the 'central determinant' of its allocation to individual schools in the scheme shall be the number and ages of pupils on roll. Beyond this, the LEA can take account of 'other factors affecting the needs of individual schools which are subject to variation from school to school', but there is a strong indication that the Secretary of State will not be prepared to approve schemes that take into account a substantial number of such factors. Indeed, in what is presumably an implicit attack on the sophisticated modes of needs analysis employed by authorities such as the ILEA, the consultative document notes that 'a multiplicity of factors will make the formula less intelligible without necessarily making it more equitable' (DES, 1988a).

Nevertheless, the document identifies two other specific factors that the Secretary of State feels ought to be included, namely the additional costs of children with special educational needs and the additional costs incurred by small schools. It is also suggested that provision might be made for different subject weightings at sixth form level and accepted that a transitional allowance may need to be made (for a maximum of four years) to deal with inherited differential patterns of expenditure. It is perhaps significant that there is no mention here of an allowance for the socioeconomic characteristics of pupils or the speed of pupil turnover, even though these were suggested in a report commissioned by the DES from management consultants Coopers & Lybrand (1988). In general, the government seems to have preferred the model employed in the Cambridgeshire experiment, despite united teacher union opposition to it in that county (Blackburne, 1988a). While the government has made some concessions in the area of special needs, it shows no positive inclination to encourage schemes that embrace the sorts of positive discrimination used in the designation of EPA/SPA schools. Furthermore, while a reduction in the number of factors used by an LEA in its formula is to be defined as a 'minor variation' not requiring the Secretary of State's approval, any addition of factors will be deemed a 'significant variation', which does require approval.

It is school governors who, while having due regard for the requirements of national and local policy, will determine the numbers of teaching and non-teaching staff that will be employed

37

in their schools and the number of incentive allowances that will be paid. Effectively, they will have the right to hire and fire staff on behalf of the LEA, even though in the case of county (as opposed to voluntary-aided) schools they will still not technically be the employers. Although the chief education officer has to be consulted in the case of the appointment of a head teacher or deputy head teacher and may make representations in other cases, the LEA will essentially be bound by the decisions of the governing body. Under section 222 of the Act, the Secretary of State will have the power to modify employment legislation to allow governing bodies of county schools to appear before industrial tribunals in place of the LEA. An LEA no-redundancy policy is apparently not binding upon governing bodies, and the costs of dismissal or premature retirement will normally have to be met by the LEA from outside the individual school's budget. As we will discuss later, it is likely that such provisions, whether intentionally or not, will reduce the effectiveness of national and local trade union agreements.

Once the LEA has determined budgetary allocations, its role under local financial management arrangements will be limited to providing guidance to governors and ensuring that schemes of delegation 'are effective in delivering better education'. LEAs will therefore maintain responsibility for appraisal and in-service training of teachers and for monitoring the performance of schools. They will also have the right to withdraw delegation as a sanction. It is interesting to consider the likely role of local authority education advisers or inspectors under the Act. This became clearer during the summer of 1988 and pronouncements from a senior DES official threw helpful light on the new relationship between central and local government in education. The advisers themselves were no doubt relieved to learn that there would indeed be a role for them, for with the clear reduction in the management function of LEAs there must have been some doubt about their future. In a speech to the National Association of Inspectors and Educational Advisers in June, Sir David Hancock, Permanent Secretary at the DES, made it clear that they would play a major role in monitoring the implementation of aspects of the Act (Surkes, 1988). Not least among these aspects would be the financial delegation procedures. Inspectors would be responsible for identifying schools where difficulties were likely to arise with regard to budgetary management.

The government recognizes that these changes will entail costs and it is making available £29.9 million in 1989–90 to cover the introduction of financial delegation and the training of governors, together with another £1.9 million for LEA inspection. Similar grant support is envisaged for the following two years. However, there is no apparent provision for the ongoing additional costs to schools of the administrative functions delegated to them. Kenneth Baker's expectation appears to be that schemes will eventually be financed out of efficiency savings and savings in central administration costs (Riddell, 1987). However, it is not necessarily envisaged that financial delegation will produce savings overall and the Coopers & Lybrand report warned that local management in schools 'should not be seen as a means of cost reduction; its purpose is to produce a more effective and responsive school system, not necessarily a cheaper one' (Coopers & Lybrand, 1988). No doubt the government would wish to make a similar case in respect of Sections 52–104 of the Act, which provide the legislative basis for the establishment of grant-maintained schools, and to which we now turn.

GRANT-MAINTAINED SCHOOLS

The 'opting out' clauses in the Act will allow the governors of any maintained secondary school and primary schools of over 300 pupils to apply to the Secretary of State to opt out of LEA control and apply to become a centrally funded grant-maintained school after a majority vote of parents in a government-funded ballot. Grant-maintained schools are presented as a response to the 'numerous indications' that the government has received 'that groups of parents want the responsibility of running their schools as individual institutions' (DES, 1987a). Since the original proposal was that schools could opt out at the whim of a simple majority of those voting, and the government resisted the successful Lords' amendment that it should be a majority of all those entitled to vote, the government was apparently not too concerned that such groups might not be representative of the parental body as a whole. Even so, the Lords vote did secure a minor concession in that, in Section 61(8), the government introduced its own amendment to require a second ballot if, on the first occasion, less than half of those eligible to vote did so. Of course, the parents of children who might want to use the school in the future have no say in the matter whatsoever, and the government has indicated that it is unlikely to consider a request that a school reverts to LEA-maintained status within ten years of the original order.

Nevertheless, the government claims that grant-maintained schools will 'add a new and powerful dimension to the ability of parents to exercise choice within the publicly provided sector of education' and that 'parents and local communities [will] have new

39

opportunities to secure the development of their schools in ways appropriate to the needs of their children and in accordance with their wishes, within the legal framework of the national curriculum' (DES 1987a). This last statement suggests that the proposal is as much about increasing central government control, at the expense of local government, as it is about increasing the power of parents and local communities. Indeed, with the demise of an LEA role in these schools, except through its right to comment on proposals and make good any deficiencies left in the service as a whole as a result of opting out, it can surely be argued that the role of the local community in relation to such schools is diminished rather than enhanced. It is true that funding levels will also be based on local LEA formulae, but before local financial management schemes are accepted, it is the Secretary of State who 'will determine an amount which he is satisfied fairly represents what the LEA would have spent on provision at the school, and on the provision of central services and benefits in relation to the school' (attachment to DES, 1988b) and deduct it from the LEA grant.

The government has made much of the fact that grant-maintained schools will not normally be permitted to change their character or admissions policies within five years of opting out, but the governors may then apply to change by publishing statutory proposals for public comment. This has been seen by critics as a backdoor means of re-introducing selection, albeit after a delay, although even that may not be necessary if there are 'changes in local circumstances' (DES, 1988b). Certainly Kenneth Baker has indicated that he would be willing to receive such proposals after five years (quoted in Hunt, 1987) and it is also the case that LEA-maintained grammar schools threatened with comprehensivization can immediately apply for grant-maintained status and receive a decision before any reorganization proposals are acted upon. They could then retain their existing character. At least one school, Tiffins Grammar in Kingston-upon-Thames, indicated that it might take this route to avoid going comprehensive (Hugill, 1987) although a change of control in the LEA removed this necessity. However, a recent report in *Education* (5 August 1988) suggests that the mere threat of Tiffins opting out has now led the LEA to give it extra resources and guarantees for its future as a selective school. The same report indicates that Wilson's Grammar School in neighbouring Sutton is now likely to be one of the first schools to set the opting out procedure in motion.

The overall extent of opting out is difficult to assess at this stage. Some observers have suggested that local financial management within an LEA context will be seen by many governing bodies as offering many of the attractions of grant-maintained status but few of the risks (McLeod, 1988). Nevertheless, there are many voluntary schools in particular which have always been ambivalent about the LEA connection and they may be encouraged in their bid for autonomy by the Grant Maintained Schools Trust, which has been established with DES support to advise schools about the procedures for making the break. Trade unions have already accused this trust of using underhand methods to encourage schools to opt out (Hugill & Garner, 1988) and Steven Norris, the chairman of the trust, has predicted that one school in every LEA in the country will be ' "free" of local authority control within the next two years' (quoted in *Education*, 5 August 1988). If this happens, others may 'feel they will have to follow, despite their deep-rooted opposition to the idea' (Horn, 1987).

CITY TECHNOLOGY COLLEGES

City technology colleges were originally announced at the 1986 Conservative party conference, before the Education Reform Act was even conceived. However, their sponsors have been granted some security and legal protection under Section 105 of the Act. Furthermore, the passage of the Bill through the House of Lords provided the occasion to broaden the concept to one of city colleges, embracing both city technology colleges (CTCs) and city colleges for the technology of the arts (CCTAs). These colleges, which are intended to provide a 'new choice of school' especially responsive to 'the changing demands of adult and working life in an advanced industrial society' (DES, 1986), can be established by an agreement between the Secretary of State and any person who undertakes to establish and maintain such schools, which will be legally independent. The schools must:

1. Be situated in an urban area.
2. Provide education for pupils of different abilities in the 11–18 age-group, drawn wholly or mainly from the area in which the school is situated.
3. Have a broad curriculum with an emphasis on science and technology, in the case of a CTC, or on technology in its application to the performing and creative arts, in the case of a CCTA.

The Act then permits the Secretary of State to contribute to both capital and current expenditure of such schools. (The Act itself does not make CTCs subject to the explicit terms of the national curriculum: see Chapter 4.)

The formulations included in the Act reflect the considerable difficulty the government has experienced in getting its original conception underway. Mr Baker's plan was that 20 such colleges should be set up, mostly in inner city areas, with their capital costs paid for by the business community. The business community has been slow to respond to the invitation to sponsor CTCs and so far only a handful have been identified. A promotional trust has been set up by the government to market the CTC initiative and the introduction of CCTAs seems to have been entirely the result of suggestions that Richard Branson, head of Virgin Records, might sponsor such an institution, which in turn would give a much-needed boost to the whole concept. In further attempts to make the initiative a success, the stress has changed to urban rather than inner city areas and the government has shown itself willing to provide up to 80 per cent of capital costs as well as 100 per cent of current expenditure. Indeed, it appears that so far the government has committed rather more to the venture than all the private sponsors so far identified, leading Jack Straw to complain that 'the government's original intention of setting up private schools with private money has now changed to setting up private schools with public money' (quoted in *Education*, 8 July 1988).

Some commentators still feel that this particular initiative remains doomed to failure. John McLeod of the Association of Metropolitan Authorities recently wrote that 'this was an initiative which local authorities did not need to frustrate: it frustrated itself through its own poor conception and inadequate preparation' (McLeod, 1988). Even so, there are those who believe that, especially when taken with grant-maintained schools, CTCs would pose a real threat to LEA provision (and, indeed, to fee-paying schools). Particularly threatening is the possibility that some existing schools, especially voluntary ones, might opt out of the maintained sector via this route. Proposals by the governors of the Haberdashers' Aske's Schools in south-east London, made public at the time the Education Reform Bill was passing through Parliament (Nash, 1988a), indicated that the CTC concept was no longer to be confined to the idea of building new schools, as in the case of the Nottingham CTC, or taking over redundant school buildings, as in the case of Solihull. It might now become a means of taking over schools that were going concerns. Indeed, Cyril Taylor, chairman of the CTC Trust, has admitted that the costs of starting schools from scratch had been 'woefully underestimated by the Department of Education and Science' and that the aim now was to 'buy up schools in use and "phase in" the CTCs over a period of up to six years' (Nash, 1988b). However, his suggestion that such schools would be based on 'the most deprived or failing school' in an

LEA has not always been borne out by the sorts of schools approached.

Something of the implications of such a development can be seen in Croydon, where (quite apart from Richard Branson's earlier interest in a site for a CCTA), Sir Philip Harris, a millionaire carpet manufacturer, is apparently interested in supporting a CTC. The head teacher and staff of Sylvan High School apparently only learnt this when they were informed that the local press would be approaching them about plans to use their school as the site for a CTC. In this case, the LEA itself appears to be centrally involved in the scheme, against the wishes of the governors. Even though it is in the top half of first-choice schools in the borough, attempts are being made by the authority's Thatcherite leaders and their supporters in the local press to portray Sylvan as an unpopular and unsuccessful comprehensive, in spite of it being praised by no less than Kenneth Baker himself as recently as 1986. In a stinging critique of the plan Gillman (1988) suggests that, although the Conservatives in Croydon echo the arguments of the Education Reform Act by claiming that the CTC will improve choice in the area,

> In fact, the opposite will be the case. At present, Sylvan is the only mixed comprehensive school in the north of the borough. Its loss will mean that local parents will no longer have that choice. Besides, there is a popular technical school, Stanley Tech, barely a mile from Sylvan, so parents already have that choice anyway.

When one has stripped away the rhetoric of the CTC initiative, one is left wondering for whom these proposals really enhance choice and to whose needs are they actually responsive. Gillman (1988) argues that in the case of Croydon:

> Any notion that the Tories are keen to help the disadvantaged is undermined by their admission that the CTC would take its 1000 pupils from a catchment area of some 5000 – restoring selection to secondary education and creating the elitist system, on the lines of the old grammar schools, that Thatcher so evidently desires.

However, we have seen that the Act implies that the children at CTCs will not be selected on the basis of 'ability', but rather according to their orientation and motivation. It will therefore be interesting to see just what sorts of pupils have been selected from the interviews with pupils and parents that are being used as a key part of the selection procedure in Solihull, where the first CTC is opening in September 1988 (Meikle, 1987).

Open enrolment, financial delegation, grant-maintained schools and city colleges are, of course, not the only structural changes introduced into the education system by the Education Reform Act. Although not the subject of this chapter, the transfer of polytechnics and major colleges of higher education out of LEA control under Sections 120–138 of the Act, proposals for financial delegation and government in LEA Colleges of Further Education under Sections 139–155, and the complete abolition of the Inner London Education Authority under Sections 162–196 reflect similar basic themes. In all these cases, what the government presents as removing power from unrepresentative and over-bureaucratic local authorities to make services more responsive to the consumer is seen by critics as an attempt to increase the power of central government at the expense of democratically elected local councils that have dared to resist the worst excesses of Thatcherism.

Before making an overall assessment of the potential structural impact of the various reforms discussed in this chapter on the educational system as a whole, we shall look briefly at two particular issues that illustrate how, when taken in conjunction with other recent policies, the Education Reform Act may well lead to significant changes of direction for the educational service. While to reverse many of the social democratic policies of the post-war era was clearly one of the government's intentions in launching the Act, neither example suggests that this will unambiguously be to the advantage of the education service and its clients. We look first at the potential impact of the Act on the role of the teaching unions and then at its implications for children with special educational needs.

THE ROLE OF THE TEACHING UNIONS

Members of the teaching profession will experience enormous changes in their conditions of work as a result of the Act. These upheavals will not be limited to the professional demands on them brought about by the national curriculum and assessment proposals. Even before the Act, the government had imposed in 1987 a new structure for the pay and conditions of school teachers. Most significantly, this led to the abolition of the Burnham Committee, which for some 40 years had been the body responsible for negotiating pay and conditions. Additionally, new regulations introduced the notion of 'directed hours', the 1265 hours during a year when every teacher is now directly responsible for his or her work to the head teacher. Now, within the Education Reform Act itself, there are various features that will change teachers' relationships with their employers and, in doing so, possibly undermine the capacity of teachers' trade unions to organize collectively to defend teachers' employment and conditions of service. These include the increased power of governing bodies to hire and fire and to vary staffing levels and the lack of obligation on an LEA to retain the services of a teacher who expresses opposition to working in a grant-maintained school, if that teacher's school chooses to 'opt out'. Either *de jure* in the case of grant-maintained schools, or *de facto*, in the case of county-maintained schools with delegated financial management, there will be many more 'employers' for trade unions to deal with. A further straw in the wind perhaps is the plan by Nottingham City Technology College not to recognize the main unions and instead to enter into a no-strike agreement with a staff association (Sutcliffe, 1988).

At the same time, the unions are having to confront potential 'dilution' of the profession. It had always been made clear that teachers in CTCs would not have to be qualified in the conventional sense and the existence of non-standard routes into teaching was also highlighted in the consultation paper on grant-maintained schools (DES, 1987a). In May 1988, when the debate on the Education Reform Bill was still progressing, the Secretary of State launched yet another consultative paper, a green paper on Qualified Teacher Status (DES, 1988c). Kenneth Baker put this document forward partly to tidy up anomalies in existing non-standard routes to qualified teacher status, but also with the intention of addressing the shortage of teachers in certain subjects, which is expected to worsen during the 1990s. Another example of 'bringing in market forces', this time through deregulation, the plan is to create a new route into teaching through 'licensing', which does not entail a specific period of pre-service training. This route would be open to people with appropriate alternative qualifications or experience. Despite the widespread concern about the proposals within the profession and without waiting for the end of its own consultation period, the government decided to introduce a late and largely unnoticed amendment to the Education Reform Bill, which amongst other things granted the Secretary of State powers under section 218(3) to make regulations relating to licensed teachers.

Although this is presented as a specific measure to address a particular short-term problem, the teaching unions are concerned that it may well represent the thin end of the wedge in deprofessionalizing teaching. Increasingly during the 1980s teaching had

45

been moving towards becoming an all-graduate profession. With the increased power of governors under the 1988 Act, especially in the new grant-maintained schools, there will be some temptation to employ licensed teachers as a matter of course, either because they prove cheaper to employ than trained graduates or perhaps because they have a less critical perspective on the education system than those who have experienced initial teacher education. Ironically, they will also not have been exposed to those aspects of the teacher education curriculum that the government itself has imposed via the Council for the Accreditation of Teacher Education, and it is difficult to see how this is consistent even with the government's own strategy for improving teaching quality (Reid & Newby, 1988). It could be attractive to the government that some trade unions might be unwilling to admit as members teachers who have entered the profession through the licensing route; some of the new-style governing bodies might well share the government's view.

The combination of these various measures, particularly in the broader context of the government's repeated moves to restrict the operations of all trade unions, is likely to limit further the capacity of the organized teaching profession to influence teachers' conditions of service, policy and practice in education. If that capacity had already been largely removed at national level, the effect of the Act will be to make it more difficult to sustain at local level.

SPECIAL EDUCATIONAL NEEDS

A useful insight into some of the complexities of the interrelationship between various aspects of government policy can be gained by considering the implications of the Education Reform Act for the provision of education for children with special needs. At the outset, it should be noted that very little is said about special educational needs in the Act, despite some important amendments, especially to its curriculum provisions, to take account of them. Nevertheless, with 'integration' becoming an increasing feature of 'special education' since the Warnock Report and the 1981 Education Act, the fate of children with special needs in grant-maintained schools and in LEA-maintained schools with local financial management ought to be a matter of great concern.

At present, children statemented as having special educational needs (SEN), usually attract a higher capitation allowance within overall funding. This 'extra' funding has usually been used to enable teaching to take place in smaller groups and/or to attract teachers who are specially skilled or who have particular specialisms within the field, and who would have been paid a special schools' allowance (now assimilated into main grade incentive allowances). Schools that operate under financial delegation will still be run under the auspices of the LEA and it is unlikely that (at least initially) they will have to pay from their delegated budget for support services, such as educational psychologists. On the other hand, as a result of a Lords' amendment to Section 38(3), specific mention is now made in the Act of the importance of taking into account in schemes of financial delegation 'the number of registered pupils at a school who have special educational needs and the nature of the special educational provision required to be made for them', thus reinforcing the terms of the draft circular (DES, 1988a).

While some LEAs will interpret this as referring only to children statemented in terms of the 1981 Act, most will probably define the concept of special educational needs quite broadly, especially in the light of restrictions on the number of other components permissible within the budget formula. In many cases, the additional monies will genuinely act as an encouragement for mainstream schools to attract children with special needs and to support their integration. However, there is no obvious mechanism for ensuring that the children on the basis of whose needs the extra funding is received will be 'targeted' in its spending; some schools may use the money for other purposes. Even so, in a situation of open enrolment, a school will have to balance the attraction of gaining additional funds from taking children with special educational needs against the possibility that the school will become stigmatized and thus face a reduction in its basic income through the effects of falling rolls. The new power of 'parental choice' could potentially lead to a severe reduction in the roll of a school seen to specialize in teaching children with special needs and ultimately this might even lead to closure.

Meanwhile, grant-maintained schools will have added to their school-based budget an allocation (based on the LEA's calculation of that school's share of central services) as funding for support services. They can also attract special grants for particular purposes, although these are intended to ensure comparability with LEA-maintained schools. In certain statutory areas they may also continue to make use of LEA services and they can be named by an LEA in a school attendance order for a pupil with special educational needs under the terms of the 1981 Education Act as amended by the 1988 Act. They can therefore be required to take statemented children and they will also receive enhanced funding for children with special educational needs in accordance with the local LEA's formula. Ministers have apparently recognized all along that only financial incentives will encourage grant-maintained schools to take pupils with SEN (Surkes, 1987). Some of these schools might therefore be tempted to take advantage of the extra funding they get for children with SEN and increase their intake of such children. In many cases though, their traditions would run counter to such a development and, in an increasingly competitive market, such schools would be particularly prone to pressures to improve their academic record by the careful selection of children with good potential for examination success. As a result statemented pupils might become increasingly marginalized within the school, while other children with SEN would find it increasingly difficult to obtain places. Interestingly, the right-wing Hillgate Group, which backs many of the measures in the Education Reform Act but feels they do not go far enough in creating competitive education 'markets', expects that it will be LEA schools that 'provide a substantial part of the educational provision for severely handicapped children' (Hillgate Group, 1987).

From this consideration of the case of special needs we begin to see a complex and confusing picture, illustrating the sometimes contradictory ways in which different aspects of the Act may interact. Nevertheless, it does appear that the factors that are likely to be influential in determining the nature of educational provision in any particular area are more likely to be finance and reputation than the particular educational needs of the local community. In the longer term, the effect may even be the re-legitimation of separate provision for special education, the very practice which the 1981 Act was designed to change. (This policy contradiction is discussed further in Chapter 8.)

CONCLUSION

When the first Thatcher government came to power in 1979, there was nothing to suggest that it would seek to alter significantly the structure of the education system. Its education policy at that time responded to the range of concerns and interests that have traditionally influenced the Conservative Party in Britain, even if the balance between the different strands had shifted somewhat since the days of the Heath government (Dale, 1983). Although one of the more contentious items in the new government's policy, the assisted places scheme, did involve provision of opportunities for pupils to move out of state schools into the private sector, this was hardly a radical departure, especially when seen in the context of education policy as a whole (Edwards *et al*, 1984). Indeed, the scheme was conceived more as a limited restoration of a style of education increasingly unavailable within the maintained sector as a result of comprehensivization than as a significant restructuring of the system as a whole (Fitz *et al*, 1986).

The 1988 Education Reform Act, however, could radically alter the shape and function of the state education system in the coming years. The idea behind such proposals as open enrolment and grant-maintained schools is to allow the market (or strictly a quasi-market) to discipline poor schools by putting them out of business. Unlike the planned admissions limits of the 1980 Act, which recognized a need to temper market forces with a modicum of planning, these proposals effectively give parental choice its head. While administrative chaos is likely in the short-term, the longer term outlook is one in which many of the positive benefits of the old partnership between government, local government and the teaching profession are likely to be lost, especially if Mrs Thatcher (rather than Mr Baker) is right about the number of schools that will opt out (Nash & Garner, 1987). Certainly, a resegmentation of the system and a return to selection will then become real possibilities.

Whether this is a result of conscious policy or merely the outcome of a series of apparently unrelated decisions, critics of current government policy have discerned a possible future scenario in which a clear hierarchy of schools will re-emerge (Campbell *et al*, 1987; Cordingley & Wilby, 1987). Although Bob Dunn, the Minister of State during the Bill's passage, argued that 'more and more specialized, differentiated schools' could develop 'without any one being regarded as inferior to the others' (quoted in *Education*, 8 July 1988), the history of English education makes it difficult to regard this claim as other than disingenuous (Banks, 1955). The new hierarchy of schools might run from prestigious private schools at the pinnacle, through city technology colleges (neither of which are made subject to the national curriculum by the Act), grant-maintained schools and voluntary-aided schools, to county-maintained schools at the base. This danger will be increased if grant-maintained schools eventually exercise their right to apply to the Secretary of State to change their status and then become overtly selective. In the longer term, it could even be that CTCs and grant-maintained schools will increasingly move into the private sector, thus making possible a largely privatized system based on education vouchers, which is still by no means off the agenda of the 'new right' (Hillgate Group, 1987). Some observers regard much of present policy as a massive 'softening up' exercise for the introduction of a much more extensive and genuine privatization of the system (Demaine, 1988).

In that situation, LEA or 'council' schools could again become the paupers of the system and the preserve of those unable or unwilling to compete in the market. As such, they might well become straightforward institutions of social control for the inner cities, where the primary concern of the staff will be the social welfare of young people rather than their education. There is a paradox here in that these are the very schools over which central government will have least control and where the local authority will have most responsibility. As we noted, the government itself has chosen not to deny that one outcome of its current proposals may be to increase racial segregation between schools. Yet the legitimacy of the system and the notion of an open society can still be maintained by devices such as the assisted places scheme, which ostensibly offer opportunities to 'worthy' disadvantaged pupils to 'escape' from their backgrounds, while actually (on the evidence available so far) attracting middle-class pupils and helping to increase the market appeal of the fee-paying sector (Fitz *et al*, 1986).

As a leading Conservative critic of the government's initiatives pointed out when they were first mooted, they 'all help most those children with parents best able to play the system to escape from poor schools. They do nothing for the quality of education of the majority who remain behind' (Argyropulo,1986). Furthermore, those in the inner cities may increasingly become the only groups in society receiving only the basic state provision. They may thereby become further divided even from the rest of the working-class and its political movements. In the current, virtually univer-salistic, system of state provision, it is at least possible to conceive of groups opposed to the injustices of the system combining to fight for gains that individually they could never hope to win. The atomization of decision-making that is a feature of current government policy threatens not only the negative conception of collecti-vism associated with inhuman state bureaucracies; it also consti-tutes an attack on the very notion that collective action, rather than the individual exercise of supposedly free choice in an unequal society, is a legitimate way of struggling for social justice.

Finally, it is important to recognize that, although there are numerous and often contradictory influences at work in the government's policies, its curriculum policies are not necessarily as much at variance with those on the structure of the education system as is sometimes suggested. The contrast between apparent centralization in one sphere and apparent decentralization in the other may not be the paradox it at first appears. Schools that are responsive to choices made by parents in the market are believed by the government to be more likely than those administered by state bureaucrats to produce high levels of scholastic achievement, to the benefit of both individuals and the nation. The strength of the state therefore has to be used to remove anything that interferes with this process or with the development of an appropriate sense of self and nation on the part of citizens. Thus, not only does the partnership with LEAs and teachers' trade unions need to be abandoned in favour of the discipline of the market, it also becomes imperative (at least in the short-term) to police the curriculum to ensure that the pervasive collectivist and universalistic welfare ideology of the post-war era is restrained so that support for self-help, the concept of the 'responsible' family and a common 'national identity' can be constructed. There is then, in political terms, a close connection between the national curriculum proposals and those other aspects of the Education Reform Act that we have discussed in this chapter.

REFERENCES
- Argyropulo, D.C. (1986) Inner city quality. *Times Educational Supplement*, 1 August.
- Banks, O. (1955) *Parity and Prestige in English Secondary Education*. London: Routledge and Kegan Paul.
- Blackburne, L. (1988a) Devolution may cost not save. *Times Educational Supplement*, 20 January.
- Blackburne, L. (1988b) Peers back policy on open enrolment. *Times Educational Supplement*, 13 May.
- Campbell, J. *et al* (1987) Multiplying the divisions? Intimations of education policy post-1987. *Journal of Education Policy*, vol. 2, no.4
- Coopers & Lybrand (1988) *Local Management of Schools*. A report to the Department of Education and Science.
- Cordingley, P. & Wilby, P. (1987) *Opting out of Mr Baker's Proposals*. London: Education Reform Group.
- Dale, R. (1983) Thatcherism and education. In Ahier, J. & Flude, M. (eds), *Contemporary Education Policy* London: Croom Helm.
- Demaine, J. (1988) Teachers' work, curriculum and the new right. *British Journal of Sociology of Education*, vol. 9, no.3.
- DES (1986) *City Technology Colleges: A New Choice of School*. London: DES.
- DES (1987a) *Grant Maintained Schools: Consultation Paper*. London: DES.
- DES (1987b) *Admission of Pupils to Maintained Schools*. London: DES.

- DES (1987c) *Consultation Paper on Financial Delegation*. London: DES.
- DES (1988a) *Draft Consultative Document on Financial Delegation to Schools*. London: DES.
- DES (1988b) *Draft Consultative Document on Grant Maintained Schools*. London: DES.
- DES (1988c) *Qualified Teacher Status: Consultation Document*. London: DES.
- Edwards, A. *et al.* (1984) The state and the independent sector. In Barton, L. & Walker, S. (eds), *Social Crisis and Educational Research*. London: Croom Helm.
- Fielding, H. (1987) Three into two won't go. *Times Educational Supplement*, 20 November.
- Fitz, J. *et al.* (1986) Beneficiaries, benefits and costs: an investigation of the Assisted Places Scheme. *Research Papers in Education*, vol.1, no.3.
- Gillman, P. (1988) Who sold our school? *New Statesman & Society*, 19 August.
- Hillgate Group (1987) *The Reform of British Education*. London: Claridge Press.
- Horn, J. (1987) Diving into dangerous waters. *Times Educational Supplement*, 18 December.
- Hugill, B. (1987) Grammars alerted to dangers of opting out. *Times Educational Supplement*, 19 June.
- Hugill, B. & Garner, R. (1988) Trust launches secret opting-out campaign, *Times Educational Supplement*, 1 July.
- Hunt, J. (1987) Selective entry 'possible for opt-out schools'. *Financial Times*, 30 November.
- McLeod, J. (1988) Mr Baker's demanding twins. *Education*, vol.172, no.2.
- Meikle, J. (1987) First CTC to start pupil selection tests. *Times Educational Supplement*, 14 August.
- Muffett, D. (1988) Soft at the centre. *Times Educational Supplement*, 19 August.
- Nash, I. (1988a) CTCs planned in secret. *Times Educational Supplement*, 20 May.
- Nash, I. (1988b) CTCs forced to alter tack. *Times Educational Supplement*, 17 June.
- Nash, I. & Garner, R. (1987) Baker quiets Tory fears of mass opt out. *Times Educational Supplement*, 18 September.
- Reid, K. & Newby, M. (1988) Is the Green Paper a cheap licence to teach? *Education*, vol.172, no.7.
- Riddell, P. (1987) Baker urges parents to take on educational role. *Financial Times*, 12 December.

• Surkes, S. (1987) Opting out may hurt special needs pupils. *Times Educational Supplement*, 23 October.
• Surkes, S. (1988) Inspectors hold the key to success of reforms. *Times Educational Supplement*, 24 June.
• Sutcliffe, J. (1987) Flagging under the spotlight. *Times Educational Supplement*, 18 September.
• Sutcliffe, J. (1988) CTC sponsors to ask for no-strike agreement. *Times Educational Supplement*, 24 June.
• Weekes, W. (1987) Tory fury at Heath attack on 'divisive' schools Bill. *Daily Telegraph*, 2 December.

4
The National Curriculum

David Coulby

THE BACKGROUND

As described in Chapter 1, the curriculum in primary and secondary schools in England and Wales, before the 1988 Education Act, was largely the responsibility of teachers and head teachers. In primary schools class teachers, in consultation with the head teacher and with each other, would decide what subjects should be taught, by what means, what the specific programmes of study should be and how the work should be assessed. In secondary schools, characteristically, the range of subjects to be taught and the amount of time and importance to be offered to each were largely determined by the head in consultation with colleagues. In practice, what had been taught in the past was a great determining factor in what should be taught in the future.

There were constraints on this autonomy of teachers and between 1944 and 1988 these had increased. The first main constraint on secondary teachers was the public examination boards. These were seen to provide almost a national curriculum by default for pupils in post-14 secondary education. Indeed the influence of the examination syllabuses penetrated further down the secondary school than this. However, there remained wide differences between the various examination board syllabuses and indeed teachers and heads could choose widely among the syllabuses, even of the same board. Furthermore, until the introduction of GCSE (first examined in 1988) there were two distinct awards for pupils at 16, which could lead to quite distinct syllabuses being followed within the same school.

A second set of constraints derived from LEA policies. Under growing pressure from the DES, in the early 1980s, the LEAs had, in a fairly unsystematic way, begun to monitor the curricula offered in the schools for which they were responsible. There were differences in the thoroughness with which this was done, not only between LEAs but also between LEA-maintained and voluntary-aided schools within the same authority. Some authorities had gone as far as issuing checkpoints or guidelines to outline for teachers the material that should have been covered or the stages that should have been reached by specified points in a pupil's career. The rigour with which these checkpoints were implemented depended, of course, on the commitment of heads and teachers.

Finally, at the central level, both the DES and the HMI were attempting with mounting rigour to influence the school curriculum. Following the DES's *Framework for the School Curriculum* of 1980, from 1984 onward HMI published a series of documents in the *Curriculum Matters* series, usually devoted to specific subject areas. Since all these papers could be was advisory, exemplary or exhortative, the extent to which they were influential varied widely between LEAs, schools and even teachers.

Arguments in favour of a more common or compulsory curriculum had been current for some time. In some cases they were derived from what was (often fancifully) perceived to be practice in other advanced industrial nation states. They were also argued in terms of a common culture or of bringing the curriculum under democractic control (White, 1973). Thus, by 1985 HMI were asserting:

> There is therefore a need for unity of purpose throughout the 5 to 16 age span. That unity needs also to apply across the school system as a whole if the desired range and quality of experience and learning are to have a more assured place than they do now across the country, in LEAs, in individual schools and, above all, in what is offered to individual pupils.
>
> (DES, 1985, p.5)

Although there was a degree of agreement with regard to the need for much greater curricular commonality, the issuing of the document *The National Curriculum 5–16: A Consultation Document* in July 1987 (DES and Welsh Office) was greeted with roars of disapproval from teachers, heads, LEAs and educationalists. The proposals of the document are not identical with the clauses of the Act, but a great deal remains effectively unchanged. It is not the idea of a national curriculum which has attracted protest, but the nature of the curriculum which is now being enforced, its mode of assessment and the high level of political control over it exerted centrally by the Secretary of State.

THE TERMS OF THE ACT

Since this chapter examines the legislation that relates to both the national curriculum and the associated arrangements for testing children and young people, the two sections on the terms of the

Act and on its effects are each divided into two to cover the curriculum and testing.

The curriculum A core curriculum of maths, English and science (and, in Welsh-speaking areas, Welsh) is established (Sections 1–5). In addition, foundation subjects of history, geography, technology, music, art and physical education are to be followed by all pupils in primary and secondary schools between the ages of 5 and 16. Religious education is also a compulsory subject, but, since it is not subject to national testing it is not a foundation subject (Sections 6–13). At secondary level pupils must additionally study a modern foreign language. All secondary pupils in Wales will also study Welsh. The Act gives the Secretary of State reserve powers to extend the national curriculum to the 16–18 age phase (Section 24).

The Act does not specify what percentage of school time each subject should take nor how much time should be devoted in total to core and foundation subjects. It makes clear that subsequent programmes of study and assessment targets should likewise steer clear of the amount of time to be spent on specific areas. However, in his speech on the second reading of the Bill in the Commons in December 1987, the Secretary of State did indicate that:

> We do not intend to lay down either on the face of the Bill or in any secondary legislation, the percentage of time to be spent on the different subjects. This will provide an essential flexibility, but it is our belief that it will be difficult, if not impossible, for any school to provide the national curriculum in less than 70 per cent of the time available. The remaining time will allow schools to offer other subject[s]—among them home economics, Latin, business studies, careers education, and a range of other subjects.
>
> (quoted in Haviland, 1988, p.3)

The national curriculum will not be enforced in fee-paying schools or in city technology colleges (CTCs). It does not apply at nursery level. It does not necessarily apply to pupils in special schools. It is recognized that some pupils with special needs in mainstream schools may have to follow a modified version of the national curriculum. Even those children without statements may follow a modified curriculum at the discretion of the head teacher, but only for six months (Sections 18–19).

Three new bodies are established, the National Curriculum Council, the Curriculum Council for Wales and the School Examinations and Assessment Council (Sections 14–15). These bodies are appointed by the Secretary of State. Their duties are to advise the Secretary of State, with whom final decisions rest, on matters concerning curriculum and assessment.

Testing   Attainment targets are to be established for the core and foundation subjects (Sections 1–4). This will be the work of the new councils mentioned above, although some of the work has been begun by the four task groups established while the Bill was still going through Parliament. These task groups were established to look at the science and technology, maths and English curriculum areas and at assessment and testing. Pupils are to be assessed against attainment targets at four 'key stages', which are effectively at the ages of 7, 11, 14 and 16.

The Act does not specify the attainment targets nor does it provide details on the publication of the test results. While the Bill was still in Parliament two reports were received from one of the task groups, that on assessment and testing (TGAT). These reports made clear recommendations on crucial assessment issues, including the publication of results (TGAT, 1987, 1988). TGAT recommended that at age 7 publication of the test results should be only to the parents of the pupil concerned, but that this decision might be at the discretion of each school. At the three other key stages schools and LEAs should publish the aggregated results of the tests. There was some conflict between the Secretary of State and the Prime Minister over the recommendations of the first TGAT report (see below), but it seems that, at least with regard to the publication of test results, the task group's advice will be followed.

THE EFFECTS OF THE ACT

The curriculum   The legislation on the curriculum represents a significant change in the organization of education in England and Wales. The curriculum is now determined by national legislation and by the Secretary of State. This power is not confined to the general shape of the school curriculum. The Act specifically states that:

> The Secretary of State may by order specify in relation to each of the foundation subjects—
> (a) such attainment targets;
> (b) such programmes of study; and
> (c) such assessment arrangements,
> as he [*sic*] considers appropriate for that subject.

> (Education Reform Act 1988 p.3)

The three councils are only advisory in their capacity. Furthermore, since they are appointed specifically by the Secretary of State, they are unlikely to veer too far into heterodoxy. The Prime

Minister herself has already been seen to intervene to block the appointment to the National Curriculum Council of people whom she considers to be politically of different persuasions from herself.

The curriculum of England and Wales has passed into central government control. There are undoubted advantages to this move. In addition to looking at these, this section will briefly examine claims to control school knowledge, analyse the nature of the knowledge that is currently enforced and consider the likely effects as it is implemented in primary and secondary schools.

As the consultation document indicated, an advantage of the national curriculum is that it will 'secure that the curriculum offered in all maintained schools has sufficient in common to enable children to move from one area of the country to another with minimum disruption to their education' (DES and Welsh Office, 1987). Children moving between schools had previously risked leaving major gaps in their curriculum progress or, alternatively, having considerable amounts of unnecessary repetition. In urban areas, with often highly mobile populations, this had served to disadvantage particular children. The difficulty occurred not just through pupils' mobility; similar gaps and overlaps occurred when teachers were changed in the course of the school year. In schools that lacked any firm central curriculum planning, gaps and repetitions could even occur as pupils progressed from one year (and thus, in primary schools, from one teacher) to another. The high mobility of the teaching force in urban areas served, in this respect, to disadvantage inner city schools. A clear national curriculum with progressive stages followed by all teachers in all schools may well serve to reduce a great many of these difficulties.

While it is necessary to remain suspicious of the current rhetoric of standards and the 'ineffective teacher' demonology, it cannot be pretended that in 1988 there were not schools and teachers whose curriculum planning left something to be desired. Many curricula and associated teaching methods were far from the best practice that had been developed in some schools. One of the aspirations of the consultation document was that the national curriculum would ensure that 'all pupils, regardless of sex, ethnic origin and geographical location, have access to broadly the same good and relevant curriculum and programmes of study which include the key content, skills and processes which they need to learn' (DES and Welsh Office, 1987). Whatever its effects on the more successful teachers (whose imagination, flair and responsiveness to local conditions are likely to be stifled), it is possible that the implementation of the national curriculum will ensure at least a minimal level of coverage of agreed subjects for all pupils.

58

It is not the place here to go into a lengthy discussion of who has the right to determine what should be school knowledge. In a democracy politically contentious issues are settled by means of elections. It is undeniable, if regrettable, that the curriculum has become politically contentious. The democratic mandate is, however, equally relevant at a local as a national level. Local authorities are not only democratically elected but also likely to be more responsive than central government to local interests, needs and circumstances. The Act severely restricts the educational role of local authorities while at the same time extending the powers of non-elected governors and enhancing the membership on such bodies of employers in particular. It is then reasonable to argue that the Act

> marks a step back from the electoral principle; in place of the universal provision of education by elected local authorities, it sets in train the differential provision of education by appointed bodies in which the elected element is in the minority and a specific group in the community is accorded a privileged place in appointments.

> (Patrick McAuslan, quoted in Haviland, 1988, p.267)

While this can certainly be argued of the Act in general, with regard to the control of the curriculum the case is less readily made. The control of the curriculum rests firmly with the democratically elected Secretary of State. Of course, it could be argued that there are other issues of considerably more interest to the electorate in a general election than, say, the relative merits of home economics as against geography in the school curriculum. But the multi-issue election is a commonly accepted aspect of the democratic system and the school curriculum is no more entitled to special pleading than any other important aspect of social policy.

However, it remains the case that with the passing of the 1988 Education Act the politicization of the school curriculum has been dramatically increased. What has been selected by Baker and his colleagues is a safely conservative school curriculum but a more radically Conservative or, for that matter, radically Labour curriculum could now be implemented by whatever Secretary of State came into power. The National Association of Head Teachers made this point in their responses to the 1987 consultation document:

> We are seriously concerned that the Secretary of State is setting a dangerous precedent which will allow future, and

possibly extremist, governments to introduce doctrinaire curricula into our schools.

(NAHT, quoted in Haviland, 1988, p.271)

As well as opening the curriculum to extremism, the Act would enable dramatic changes to take place in what is taught in schools. The curriculum might swing from, on the one hand, compulsory Christianity, anti-gay indoctrination, nationalist history and literature, Latin and arithmetic to, on the other hand, anti-racist and anti-sexist studies, peace studies, heritage languages, atheist education and lessons in gay rights. Dramatic curricular shifts with each change of government and significant curricular change with each new Secretary of State are now a likelihood. Once the secret garden is unlocked predatory politicians of all parties are free to roam.

The matter of expertise is also at issue, since the detailed content of the curriculum is prescribed not by the NCC or specialist working groups but by the Secretary of State himself. When the working groups on maths and science issued their final reports (DES, 1988a,b), Secretary of State Baker felt free to accept the portions he liked but to revise those with which he disagreed. On this occasion an editorial in *The Times Educational Supplement* was prompted to object:

> The real question which underlies this whole exercise is not whether Mr Baker or the experts are right, but why we should be expected to accept him as the arbiter of science education (or long division) rather than them? Many people will feel that what is happening exemplifies the basic objection to the national curriculum that it puts the power of decision on professional matters in the hands of laymen [sic] with strong prejudices and little knowledge.

(TES, 19 August 1988, p.3)

It is worth quoting John White on the content of the national curriculum: 'There is no virtue in a national curriculum as such. Hitler had a national curriculum, and so did Stalin. The basic issue is: what kind of national curriculum is Mr Baker giving us?' (White, 1988, p.120). In fact the curriculum that has been favoured is very much that of the old grammar school. It is traditional both in its selection and in its fragmentation. This point is vividly illustrated by Richard Aldrich (1988):

> To an historian the most striking feature of the national curriculum is that it is at least 83 years old. State secondary schools were established by the 1902 Act and in 1904 the

Board of Education issued regulations which prescribed the syllabus for pupils up to the ages of sixteen or seventeen in such schools.

Aldrich then tabulates the two legislated curricula. English, maths, science, history, physical education and geography appear in both. The foreign language of 1904 has become the modern foreign language of 1987, drawing has become art, manual work/housewifery has become technology and only music in the 1988 curriculum is not included in that of 1904. Aldrich observes:

> There is such a striking similarity between these two lists that it appears that one was simply copied from the other, although the term 'modern foreign language' in the 1987 list excludes Latin which featured prominently in the secondary school curricula of 1904.... Thus in essence the proposed national curriculum in so far as it is expressed in terms of core and foundation subjects, appears as a reassertion of the basic grammar school curriculum devised at the beginning of the twentieth century by such men as Robert Morant and James Headlam.... This curriculum is now to be extended to primary and comprehensive secondary schools.
>
> (Aldrich, 1988, pp.22–3)

Embedded within this traditional and academicist selection of school knowledge is a strong right-wing and nationalist potential. Religious education is almost completely identified with the teaching of Christianity. It will be interesting to see which particular modern foreign languages are favoured and whether the languages of the various communities of England and Wales are adequately represented. As in the case of maths and science, the details in the power of the Secretary of State will also be crucial: will the programme of study for history, for example, include analysis of the economic aspects of imperialism, or will it be the saga of England's splendid victories?

Notable absentees from the list of national subjects are economics, sociology, social studies and politics. This unsurprising exclusion is in line with the distrust shown by successive Thatcher administrations for the social sciences. Social sciences (the very term has been anathematized) are seen as being dangerously left-wing and their teachers as raving Marxists almost to a person. The consultation document had insisted that the national curriculum would raise standards in the area of education linked to adult life. It is hard to see how responsible, participating democratic citizens can be educated if their curriculum deliberately excludes all issues relating to political, economic and social thinking. John White makes the point more strongly:

> Indoctrination is basically to do with preventing reflection. Directly inculcating doctrines is only one way of doing this.... A most powerful way of indoctrinating pupils is by so organising their studies that certain kinds of reflection—about political matters, for instance—are off the agenda. This was not possible for governments to achieve directly before the recent shift from professional control of curricula; but now, by filling school timetables with safe subjects, by determining much of the syllabuses to be covered, and by focussing teachers' attention on getting pupils through national tests, preventing thought about fundamental values is a much more feasible task.
>
> (White, 1988, pp.121–2)

More surprising is the exclusion of home economics from the national curriculum. Again this is an area where pupils can see the immediate relevance of their studies to their own lives, one of the proclaimed aims of the consultation document. Indeed it is a subject not without application to those Victorian values beloved by the Prime Minister herself. Perhaps its recent non-sexist, practical and critical incarnation has placed home economics, with other social sciences, on the outer curriculum margins.

The academicism of the national curriculum separates it in other ways too from both adult life and the world of work. Certainly it is encouraging to see technology included as a foundation subject at both primary and secondary levels. However, the national curriculum contains no specific reference to computing, to microprocessors or to information technology: business studies and commercial studies are also surprisingly excluded. Recent innovations in the secondary curriculum under the auspices of the (Training Commission funded) Technical and Vocational Educational Initiative (TVEI) may well be endangered by these exclusions. The Confederation of British Industry made similar points in its response to the consultation document. The CBI expressed its concern that:

> the document does not contain any specific reference relating to economic awareness and understanding, or careers education. It is important that the national curriculum allows sufficient scope for adequate coverage of aspects of educational experience outside the narrow confines of the traditional individual subject disciplines.
>
> (CBI, quoted in Haviland, 1988, pp.29–30)

Much depends on the programmes of study that are ultimately approved for the technology foundation area and the status which, as a non-core subject, it achieves within the curriculum. In the light of an imputed link between an irrelevant school curriculum and youth unemployment (see Chapter 1) the adoption of a traditional grammar school curriculum, devoid of any vocational elements, must be seen as a major inconsistency on the part of the government.

It is important to recognize that the implementation of the national curriculum in schools reflects grammar school tradition in the further sense that its orientation is exclusively towards secondary style disintegrated subjects. This may prove difficult for primary schools, with their more integrated topic-work approach. In their response to the consultation document the Conservative Education Association, no less, expressed concern at the secondary orientation of the proposed national curriculum:

> It would be regrettable if the proposed national curriculum were to be interpreted as curtailing rather than encouraging, the good practice existing in our best primary schools.

> (CEA, quoted in Haviland, 1988, p.41)

In fact integrated work has also become an important aspect of good secondary practice, and here too progress may be reversed. These anxieties may be allayed as the programmes of study and attainment targets are published by the task groups and the NCC. There are actually encouraging signs in, for instance, the *Interim Report* of the Science Working Group, where the integrated nature of much primary science teaching is recognized:

> Teachers may include science and technology in general topics which cover a number of subject areas and may occupy a large part of the curriculum without being identified in terms of separate subjects.... Science and technology may be learned in activities which do not necessarily begin from a science-based focus, but might be such as the study of an old building, the postal system or a seasonal festival.

> (Science Working Group, 1987, p.38)

This is an encouraging contrast with the initial consultation document. However, the explicit statements on the face of the Act do nothing to encourage the view that integrated studies will continue to thrive. For schools, especially at primary level, this could prove to be a most retrograde step. The pressure of impending assessment points may force them to abandon the flexibility and adaptability of their integrated approach in order to ape the subject-based timetables of traditional grammar schools.

Primary schools seem particularly vulnerable to possibly unintended consequences of the national curriculum in other ways too. While most primary schools cover most elements of the core and foundation subjects at present, technology is an area which has yet to gain appropriate prominence in their curricula. Some of the advantages of the more widespread introduction of technology may be lost if it is seen as a single one-off subject rather than as another, though vital, component of the integrated primary curriculum. Primary schools have developed good practice with regard to utilizing local facilities and opportunities. Schools have endeavoured to reflect in their curricula the industrial, commercial, cultural and topographical aspects of their surrounding localities. A crucial aspect of such work in the multicultural curriculum has been the inclusion of elements reflecting the various languages, religions and traditions of contemporary UK. Too tight an emphasis on *national* programmes of study would inhibit primary schools' effectiveness in responding to *local* circumstances. These fears are particularly well justified with regard to multicultural studies, where the promotion of one of Britain's religions over the others in the school curriculum is explicit in the Act.

It is possible that, for many secondary schools, the implementation of the national curriculum will have less profound effects than in the primary sector. The GCSE exam system already provides a framework of externally defined curriculum constraints for 14–16-year-olds. Many secondary schools spend much of their time teaching disintegrated subjects which include those prescribed in the national curriculum. Some subjects will be taught more widely: five years of history and geography are far from common at present, as are five years of a modern foreign language. Other subjects, particularly social studies, home economics and practical and vocational subjects, will have a hard fight to retain their places in the timetable. The possible loss of some of the TVEI initiatives has been mentioned above. The other major change in the 14–16 curriculum in recent years has been the introduction of the GCSE exams. There are indications in both the consultation documents and the TGAT reports that the government and its advisers are not completely happy with the provision of this new exam. The consultation document, for instance, asserted that 'not all GCSE criteria are sufficiently specific' (DES and Welsh Office, 1987, p.10). Before the first cohort of pupils had even taken the examinations the possibility began to be voiced that, under the national curriculum, further major changes might be needed. If such changes were implemented they could not but lead to a further period of destabilization in secondary schools.

Although the national curriculum is currently confined to the 5–16 age group, the Act gives reserve powers to the Secretary of State to extend its remit to the post-compulsory years, to FE colleges and to PCFC institutions. The national curriculum could then be used to introduce, from central government, sweeping changes in the curriculum of young people in the post-compulsory sector of education.

A difficulty that will affect the implementation of the national curriculum at both primary and secondary levels is the supply of teachers. In order for modern languages to be taught to all secondary pupils for five years many more specialist teachers will be needed. A recent consultation document (DES, 1988c) implies that the government hopes to be able to recruit some of these teachers directly from the EC. Similarly, if all primary pupils are to study technology for six years, then all—or nearly all—primary teachers will need to be able to teach it. Since this is far from the case at present a large-scale INSET (inservice education of teachers) programme will be required, as well as some significant changes in initial primary teacher education. The new assessment arrangements will, further, require at both primary and secondary level skills from teachers and head teachers which few of them now possess. Again a large-scale and expensive INSET operation will be necessary before these arrangements can be effectively implemented. The second TGAT report attempted to minimize the difficulties in this respect and advocated the cascade model, already partially discredited from its use in the introduction of GCSE. If sufficient attention is not paid to INSET and appropriate resources are not made available, it will be easy to predict that the assessment arrangements crucial to the national curriculum will not be effectively implemented. The next section considers these arrangements in more detail.

The consultation document invoked the ugly spectre of parents joining HMI in scrutinizing the works of schools and teachers in order to report any 'deviation from set text' to the Secretary of State. The Act is less forthright about this, although the Secretary of State is given extensive powers to obtain information from schools. Some scrutiny of the national curriculum will be necessary and it may be that HMI will find themselves with the unfortunate task of going round schools (as they have already gone round colleges, polytechnics and universities) counting how many hours of which subject are being taught to ensure that they comply with the terms of the national curriculum.

Testing While the Education Bill was passing through Parliament, many in the education world were cheered by the publication of the first report from TGAT. Unlike the consultation document, which the Bill was to enable, the TGAT report advocated a more sophisticated assessment pattern:

> The assessment process itself should not determine what is to be taught and learned.... For the purpose of national assessment we give priority to the following four criteria:
> —the assessment results should give direct information about pupils' achievement in relation to objectives: they should be *criterion-referenced*;
> —the results should provide a basis for decisions about pupils' further learning needs: they should be *formative*;
> —the scales or grades should be capable of comparison across classes and schools, if teachers, pupils and parents are to share a common language and common standards: so the assessments should be calibrated or *moderated*;
> —the ways in which criteria are set up and used should relate to expected routes of educational development, giving some continuity to a pupil's assessment at different ages: the assessments should relate to *progression*.

> (TGAT, 1987, paragraphs 4 and 5)

The report emphasized the formative aspects of assessment. A range of assessment approaches, delivered and marked by teachers, were advocated against short sharp standardized tests. The report further recommended that the results of the tests at 7 should only be published to parents (although this has subsequently become less clear since schools are to be given discretion about publication at this stage). Of course it was the allaying of some of the earlier anxieties rather than the establishment of a national testing bureaucracy that cheered educationalists.

The Secretary of State warmly welcomed the TGAT report, which seemed not only to make his aims realizable but also to be less unacceptable to the profession than had earlier been anticipated. Its positive and clear recommendations contrasted with the less helpful (to him) earlier report from the Mathematics Working Group (1987). However, it subsequently transpired, via a leaked letter from her private office, that the Prime Minister was far from happy with the TGAT recommendations. She recognized that these would lead to a costly testing apparatus; leave authority with teachers (even worse, 'she is also concerned to note the major role envisaged for LEAs in the implementation of the system' (*The*

Independent, 10 March 1988, p.1); take a considerable amount of time to implement and not provide the clear public yardstick of cost effectiveness for which she was looking. The Prime Minister did want short, sharp, cheap, nationally administered tests with clear, league-table-style published results. By June 1988, when in a parliamentary written answer (Baker, 1988) the Secretary of State was able to announce the government's adoption of many of the TGAT recommendations, it seemed as if he had won this particular battle. However, the tensions between the Baker and the Thatcher views of testing will only be resolved as the Act is implemented. The Prime Minister's concern with cost may in the event be a crucial influence.

Of all the proposals relating to the national curriculum, it is those concerning the publication of the test results that have provoked the most serious public and professional outcry. Regular, systematic assessment of pupils to judge their progress and to ensure the appropriateness of the curriculum work they are doing is an indispensable element of successful teaching. Few teachers would object to the stipulation of regular assessment or even perhaps to the establishment of national criteria or guidelines. There is also an accepted place for regular feedback to parents so that they can be aware of their children's progress, or lack of it. However, this is by no means the same as a general publication of results. As the Church of England Board of Education protested in its response to the consultation document:

> Those whose success in life have [sic] brought them to the position of being policy makers can have little real idea of the debilitating effect of being publicly labelled a failure at any age, let alone twice within the period of one's primary schooling.
>
> (quoted in Haviland, 1988, p.98)

In their response the Rathbone Society spelt out some of the specific effects:

> For the child with learning difficulties they [the tests] will serve to reinforce failure. This, in turn, will lead to an increasing lack of self-confidence and self-esteem, qualities which all children need and which are fundamental requirements of employers.
>
> (quoted in Haviland, 1988, p.94)

The insistence that test results should be published is an attempt to introduce cost-indicators and competition into the education system. Published results would allow the consumers (presumably parents) to measure the effectiveness of school against school, teacher against teacher. Parents would then be able to express their choice by patronizing successful schools and teachers and by transferring their pupils from the unsuccessful (open enrolment— see Chapter 3—being simultaneously enacted to facilitate such transfers). Within this scenario the successful schools would grow and thrive and the unsuccesful sink into decline and decay. A side-effect of this development, doubtless attractive to the policy makers, is that the ethos of competition, central to capitalist ideology, will be encouraged in many areas. Schools will compete against schools, teachers against teachers, pupils against pupils. Whatever else children and young people learn from the national curriculum they will learn the importance, and presumably the intrinsic rightness, of competition.

In fact these are not the likely effects of the publication of results. The absolute results of pupils do not provide an adequate output measure for schools. There are major differences between schools in the skills, interests and motivations of their pupils. Schools have different buildings and equipment, staffing levels and funding. To measure test result outputs independently of such variables is not in any way to compare like with like. If parents do pay attention to the published test results when they are selecting schools for their children, then the pressure of low recruitment is likely to fall on those disadvantaged schools and those which take a preponderance of pupils with learning difficulties. It is likely that some parents will not use the tests as their basis for selection. Those middle-class parents who do use them in this way have had little difficulty in selecting the most privileged schools for their children in the past, without the benefit of published test results. These matters are discussed at greater length in Chapters 8 and 9.

As the Rathbone Society response quoted above makes clear, a certain effect of the publication of results will be that many children are labelled as failures at an early age. The self-fulfilling aspects of this labelling process are well and widely known (Hargreaves *et al*, 1975). Children will be stratified in their own eyes and those of their peers, teachers and parents. The risks to the motivation of the least successful are profound. Far from increasing school effectiveness and raising standards by encouraging competition, the publication of results will lead to spurious comparisons between schools and to disappointment, demotivation and frustration for many pupils. The recommendations of the TGAT reports do little to mitigate these effects, beyond suggesting, and then only half-heartedly, that the results of the tests at 7 should not be published. At 11 such publication is apparently satisfactory.

In the past one of the effects of widespread testing, such as the eleven-plus, is that the prospect of the test has had an inhibiting effect on the curriculum that precedes it. Standardized tests are seen to narrow teachers' and pupils' objectives and lead to narrowness within the curriculum. The national curriculum itself represents a severe restriction on what can be taught in schools. It is the job of the NCC and the SEAC to ensure that the attainment targets and the mode and range of recommended assessment do not further impoverish and restrict what is taught in schools. The assessment must reflect the full range of the national curriculum and be an aid rather than an obstruction to its effective teaching and learning.

Despite TGAT's disclaimers, it is likely that expenditure on the testing apparatus will be considerable. The testing bureaucracy will need to be established and developed at national and local levels. Large amounts of specialist time will be needed to develop and pilot the assessment materials. Teachers and head teachers will need substantial INSET work. The setting, marking and moderating of tests and the feeding back of results will involve considerable amounts of teacher time. The costs of all these activities taken together will be substantial. Primary teachers with 40 pupils in delapidated, under-equipped classrooms or secondary head teachers with no maths graduates on the staff might well question whether such expenditure represents the most appropriate use of educational resources.

CONCLUSION

Change in education is notoriously difficult to implement. Some of the changes in the national curriculum section of the 1988 Act, especially those concerned with the publication of results or those which might imply any premature revision of GCSE, are deeply unpopular with teachers, heads and LEA advisors. The profession as a whole has little reason to offer Baker its support: apart from being the man who deprived them of their negotiating rights, he is regarded as a politician more interested in furthering his own career than in the painstaking implementation of important educational change. These changes, then, may well evoke considerable professional resistance or at least foot-dragging.

The reports of the working parties are taking time to come in. They have to be considered by the NCC, not to mention the Secretary of State; they will have to be revised and correlated one with another. Programmes of study and attainment targets for all core and foundation subjects will take years to finalize. Even in the wake of the Prime Minister's displeasure, TGAT's second report still envisaged a period of four years before the assessment arrangements could be completely implemented.

The national curriculum will offer security for some heads and teachers and a potentially monotonous routine to others. Opted out schools might be more resolute in adopting the national curriculum as a means of proving their effectiveness (not to mention pleasing their new purse-bearer at the DES) and thereby attracting more of the type of pupils whom they would see as contributing to their further success. This, in turn, would put pressure on the schools in the LEA sector. The notion of a national curriculum probably carries some degree of consensus. Certainly during the debate in Parliament there were no statements from the opposition to give any impression but that a national curriculum—though not necessarily this one—is here to stay. It would be a mistake to imagine that this chapter of the Act will not be effectively implemented, but it will certainly not all be implemented immediately.

REFERENCES

• Aldrich, R. (1988) The national curriculum: an historical perspective. In Lawton, D. & Chitty, C. (eds), *The National Curriculum*. London: Institute of Education.

• Baker, K. (1988) Parliamentary written answer to Mr. Robert Key, 7 June 1988.

• DES (HMI) (1985) *The Curriculum from 5 to 16: Curriculum Matters 2*. London: DES.

• DES and Welsh Office (1980) *A Framework for the School Curriculum*. London: DES.

• DES and Welsh Office (1987) *The National Curriculum 5–16: Consultation Document*. London: DES.

• DES (1988a) *Mathematics for Ages 5 to 16*. London: DES.

• DES (1988b) *Science for Ages 5 to 16*. London: DES.

• DES (1988c) *Qualified Teacher Status: Consultation Document*. London: DES.

• Hargreaves, D.H. *et al*. (1975) *Deviance in Classrooms*. London: Routledge.

• Haviland, J. (ed.) (1988) *Take Care Mr Baker! The Advice on Education Reform Which the Government Collected But Withheld*. London: Fourth Estate.

• Mathematics Working Group (1987) *Interim Report*. London: DES.

• Science Working Group (1987) *Interim Report*. London: DES.

- Task Group on Assessment and Testing (1987) *A Report.* London: DES.
- Task Group on Assessment and Testing (1988) *Three Supplementary Reports.* London: DES.
- White, J.P. (1973) *Towards a Compulsory Curriculum.* London: Routledge.
- White, J. (1988) An unconstitutional national curriculum. In Lawton, D. & Chitty, C. (eds), *The National Curriculum.* London: Institute of Education.

5
Further Education and the Control of Youth

Leslie Bash

THE BACKGROUND

Conventionally, colleges of further education have performed the function of servicing industry and commerce in the UK through the provision of vocational courses on a part-time or full-time basis. Such courses, together with work-based apprenticeships, have constituted what might be regarded as the vocational training system. It was, it must be admitted, a system concerned with a minority of young people. Traditionally, it provided education and training for the male half of the youth population and then only those involved with what have been termed skilled occupations.

In order to appreciate the context of that part of the Act dealing with further education, there is a need to examine some of the fundamental changes which have affected this entire sector of the population in addition to government policy responses. In short, during the past 15 years, there has been an increasing focus upon what some people regard as the most problematic segment of the population: the nation's youth.

Both structural and cultural factors have been highly significant. In addition to important shifts in the economy and in employment opportunities for young people during the past 15 years, there has also been a change in the size of the youth population. The country has moved from a situation of a rising number of young people in the 16–19 age group to one of decline. Paradoxically, though, youth unemployment remains, alongside a growing shortage of skilled workers. This may be partially explained by a decrease over the past few years in the proportion of 16-year-olds staying on at school after their fifth year (*Times Educational Supplement*, 17 June 1988). One consequence, however, of the declining 16–19 population is an increase in the proportion obtaining employment, the result of which is already having knock-on effects on the Youth Training Scheme (discussed later). In Berkshire, for example, it has been reported that many employers prefer to run their own training schemes, offering trainees

72

relatively good rates of pay (*Times Educational Supplement*, 29 July 1988).

At the same time expressions of frustration and collective identity became manifest in the growing disturbances in inner cities (and, more lately, in suburban and rural areas) and football hooliganism. Yet again, youth is perceived as a threat to the social order, echoing the moral panics of the past 100 years and the subsequent responses of government, religious and other organizations to control their behaviour (Bash *et al.*, 1985, p.57).

What appears to have happened in the 1980s, however, is that in addition to the usual exhortations to young people to behave responsibly and the calls for tougher penal measures, the established education authorities have come under fire for having failed Britain's youth. It is within this context that the intervention by the central state through non-educational agencies, in a bid to change the very manner in which young people are perceived and treated in society, becomes significant. There is a view that the young have achieved a prominence out of all proportion to their economic importance; that their culture (sex, drugs and rock 'n' roll) has become dominant, much to the detriment of the social, economic and moral health of the nation.

The new thinking on the treatment of the 16–19 population has reflected not only the concerns of the right but also some of the misgivings of the left regarding existing arrangements for the school–work transition. Not only have assumptions concerning the employment of young people been severely challenged, but also their very status in society has come under scrutiny. Thus, it was not to be the arm of central government dealing with education policy that was to guide developments in this sphere but the employment service. The former Manpower Services Commission has become the leading player, replacing educational concerns by concerns with unemployment, training and the right to welfare benefits. This last point is crucial to the status of young people: the new Social Security regulations (April 1988) among other things will have the effect of further encouraging participation in training schemes if immediate employment is unavailable, since Income Support (replacing Supplementary Benefit) will not be payable to school-leavers.

The central state has, therefore, apparently been able to deal with the potential threat of a disenchanted youth population in a relatively short space of time. On the surface, the policies enacted may seem to be pragmatic responses to immediate difficulties (unemployment, urban disorder) but, on further examination, they constitute a clear ideological position. This can be seen in the notion of *vocationalism*. It should be noted that vocationalism is not equivalent to the idea of vocational education, which, at least in theory, could have relevance for all young people, providing them with a sound basis for understanding the world of work and preparing them for employment at all levels. Rather, it operates as an ideology, perpetuating the work ethic even where work itself might be unavailable for large numbers of school-leavers. In practice, vocationalism indicates the maintenance of a social hierarchy where the fortunate few may continue with their education in the sixth forms of those schools which manage to survive and even prosper in the wake of falling rolls, grant-maintained status and so-called freedom of choice. The rest, apart from those able to find immediate employment, are absorbed into training schemes and vocational preparation courses based with employers, in FE colleges and in other institutions.

The education of young people beyond compulsory schooling has tended to reflect the divisions within society: class, gender and, more recently, race. Indeed, the education of the 16–19-year-old population has always comprised a *pot-pourri* of academic elitism and vocational training, reflecting on the one hand the *ad hoc* development of technical and vocational education, and on the other the prevailing class ideology. The public and grammar schools retained their most promising pupils until 18 or 19, providing them with a sponsored route to university and the professions. Further education generally provided the—overwhelmingly male—skilled working-class with the necessary licences to practise their crafts. The sole countervailing trend has been for some authorities to promote the idea of tertiary colleges during the 1970s, incorporating school sixth form and further education provision. The comprehensivization of 16–19 (even 16 plus) education, although sometimes brought in to cut the cost of A level provision in a wide number of institutions, was a move in the direction of greater educational democracy. It suggested that 16–19 general and vocational education need not be provided along segregated lines and that there was little basis for a stratified education system other than to sponsor the reproduction of divisions in society at large.

Despite moves by some metropolitan LEAs towards a tertiary policy, the stratification of 16–19 provision gathered apace. With structural changes in employment and the recession of the 1970s, opportunities for conventional training in skilled manual trades declined and further education underwent a partial metamorphosis. To a large degree it had the function of providing some kind of schooling for those young people left out in the cold—what might simply be called vocationalism.

It is evident that whatever particular merits vocationalism might have in practice, and there are many who suggest that it has opened up avenues for future employment for a large number of working-class children, it is essentially ideological in character. As such, the changes of the past 10 years or so should be viewed as a collection of responses to social change and social disruption rather than to the demands of the economy. While the demand from school-leavers has continued to be articulated in terms of jobs, the central government response has been to devise a succession of holding operations based on the popularly held view that young people need to be prepared for a rapidly changing world of work. Although the vocationalism of recent years provides a backdrop to the changes in further education contained in the 1988 Act, especially the increased role played by employers in college governance, the vexed relationship between industry and education as a whole provides an even broader context.

Conventional wisdom now decrees that the education received by most school-leavers has ill-prepared them for a world of ever-changing technology and an equally rapidly changing occupational structure. It is argued that the schools and universities have been overly concerned with abstract knowledge while the further education sector has been wedded to a past world of apprenticeships for a privileged minority of working-class youth. Apparently, the time is seen to be right for a new orientation in education. But while the schools get back to basics via the national curriculum and the higher education sector more directly serves the needs of industry, further education institutions have the opportunity to perform an essential preparatory function. Current government policy is consequently based upon a view of a rapidly changing economy associated with an acceleration in technological development. Essentially, it is suggested that school-leavers can no longer plan their careers with any degree of certainty and that they should be prepared to be *flexible* in their approach. The education provided for 16–19-year-olds must therefore reflect this uncertainty through an emphasis on greater flexibility in both teaching and learning.

There is little doubt that the Youth Training Scheme is the flagship of this policy and although it has received wide publicity, a brief description is appropriate. Launched by the Manpower Services Commission as part of an overall training policy (the New Training Initiative), it guaranteed a place to every 16-year-old school-leaver, to some 17-year-olds, and to older people with

75

disabilities. As with the previous Youth Opportunities Programme it involved the two elements of work experience and work preparation but in this case the two elements were to be seen as part of a one-year integrated programme of training for the world of work. Essentially, YTS was to be a 12-month programme of practical work-based training (including three months off-the-job) with a weekly allowance paid. A significant aspect of the scheme was the different modes of operation: either employer-based (with placement for off-the-job training) or college/workshop based (with placement with employers for work experience). The latter mode seemed particularly well suited to young people with special educational needs.

Unlike previous schemes, YTS was intended as a permanent aspect of the further education and training system. In 1985 it was announced that the scheme was to be extended from one year to two and that it would lead to a nationally recognized vocational qualification. It would encompass, eventually, all programmes of initial post-16 vocational training and include the first years of apprenticeship. However, the YTS structure also underwent change, with greater power given to employers as a result of the scrapping of the college-based mode of operation.

Within the context of the decline in manufacturing industry and the accelerating changes in those industries that remain, YTS has allegedly provided a radically different perspective on training. Accordingly, industrial training was no longer to be tied to narrow trade practices and ought not encourage loyalty to specific occupations. The current ideology emphasizes mobility, individualism and adaptability to technological change. Moreover, the new training was to have the task of encouraging entrepreneurship and self-improvement to prepare young people for a highly competitive world in which they must seek their own salvation.

Although the 1988 Act appears to want to distinguish very clearly the school curriculum from that of FE colleges (given the national curriculum), in practice it has not been possible to maintain such a distinction. The traditional picture, of schools as institutions devoted to the general education of young people and further education establishments as essentially concerned with vocational training, has changed significantly. On the further education scene, the growth in courses of vocational preparation has heralded the development of teaching in the areas of life and social skills and basic skills (including numeracy and literacy). Increasingly, a large part of further education is catering for young people who, whether they ultimately gain employment or not, are regarded as having special educational needs manifested in learning difficulties of one kind or another. Such students might be offered what is essentially a programme of general education designed in remedial fashion to compensate for their lack of progress in the school system.

As much of the established craft-level work of further education colleges declines as a consequence of economic change, and with it the award of standard vocational qualifications, so there is an expansion of pre-vocational or vocational preparation courses. Further education colleges are now involved with basic general education contained within a vocational framework. As a consequence, teachers in further education colleges have had to face a change in their role: no longer can they take for granted their function as specialists in particular work-related disciplines because such disciplines are frequently no longer in demand. Teachers as well as students are now being encouraged to be flexible in outlook as a result of changes in the curriculum.

The changes in the further education curriculum have had interesting consequences for the structure and organization of colleges. As non-advanced further education becomes increasingly dominated by programmes of vocational preparation so the work undertaken in that area often becomes concentrated in single departments, frequently cutting across discipline boundaries. Teachers in such departments are faced with a student population that is not destined for specific occupations (or, perhaps, any occupation). Their task then is to implement a curriculum which in practice is a continuation or a repeat of secondary schooling (and, perhaps, even of primary schooling).

Indeed, the school–further education divide has continued to be eroded. The idea of transferable learning as an essential component of preparation for the future is closely connected not only with the new vocationalist 16 plus curricula but also with the Technical and Vocational Education Initiative (TVEI). A national initiative under the control of the Department of Employment, TVEI seeks to provide a vocationally oriented curriculum for the 14–18 age group. As such, it is seen as a collaborative exercise between secondary schools, further education colleges, industry and commerce, and other interested bodies.

The aim has been not to provide an alternative curriculum for those young people deemed to be non-academic but rather to extend opportunities to become involved in activities linked with the world of work to a wide range of students irrespective of their abilities. One TVEI consortium offers a range of courses, from computing to community theatre, leading to a variety of qualifications (GCSE, City and Guilds, etc.) reflecting the potential for local variation. Such local variations suggest that LEAs, schools and colleges have a degree of freedom in the interpretation of Training Commission guidelines in relation to TVEI. Yet as Dale (1986) points out, the new FE ideology of TVEI, with its emphasis on profiling, evaluation, accountability, skill acquisition and work experience, has created a framework that places limits on local autonomy. Furthermore, a question mark must now hang over the future of TVEI given the reassertion of the power of the Secretary of State for Education over curricular matters and particularly in the light of the Newcastle University research (Times Educational Supplement, 1 July 1988). Surprisingly, TVEI pupils performed worse in the 1987 examinations than comparable non-TVEI pupils in the same schools. If these findings impress Secretaries of State who emphasize the results of tests and the award of qualifications within the context of greater uniformity in curriculum matters, then Department of Employment sponsored programmes may find themselves eased out.

Finally, there should be some mention of the Certificate of Pre-Vocational Education—an initiative controlled by local education authorities. It was seen as an option for those 16-year-olds who previously might have stayed on in the sixth form to take a few O levels (what was known as the new sixth). In an era of youth unemployment, a one-year full-time programme of vocational preparation, incorporating work experience, was viewed as preferable for those regarded as unsuitable for a traditional sixth form course. The stated aim of CPVE, like YTS, was to provide the kind of flexibility appropriate to the needs of both students and the changing economy.

Although CPVE was conceived within a vocationalist framework, the absence of Department of Employment control has made possible a degree of manoeuvre. One action-research project (Cohen, 1986) focusing on CPVE has been able to draw upon the 'so-called "active pedagogy" of the new vocationalism' to attempt to provide an alternative learning context that would counter the divisions of labour reinforced by that vocationalism. It must be said that, faced with the competition of YTS with its financial incentive, however meagre, CPVE was bound to face survival difficulties and, at the time of writing, does indeed appear to have receded into the background.

Sixteen-to-nineteen education remains highly problematic. Social divisions become manifested as educational divisions, in much the same way as they did during the heyday of selective secondary schooling. Tripartitism has now re-emerged in the tertiary sector (Gleeson, 1983) with claims that the further education

curriculum is highly segregated and that YTS provision is analo-
gous to the secondary modern school. Thus, the further education
scene, which was never a stranger to market forces, becomes even
more attractive for governments wishing to impose the market
ideology while at the same time using it as a dumping ground for
those who haven't quite made it.

Sixteen-to-nineteen education has thus been characterized by
the imposition of overt centralized control, in a way that the other
sectors of education are only now beginning to experience. This
control, in addition to not being exercised by the DES, came about
in a piecemeal if hurried manner. It was, for example, the Chancellor of the Exchequer, in his Budget speech, who announced the
two-year YTS programme to the House of Commons and it was the
Prime Minister who announced TVEI. It was as though there had
been a gradual realization, a revelation even, that vocationalism
had to be put at the top of the national political agenda. It was
certainly much too important to be left to the DES, which was
permeated both by traditionalism and by leftist progressivism in
educational thinking. However, since the 1988 Education Act was
to be all-encompassing, the 16–19-year-olds were not to be
ignored, despite the now entrenched position of the Department of
Employment.

THE TERMS OF THE ACT

In many respects, the 1988 Education Act devotes comparatively
little space to further education, although this is not altogether
surprising. Historically, technical and vocational education has
not been at the forefront of educational policy in this country.
However, the 1944 Act did enjoin local education authorities to
secure not only the availability of selective secondary schooling
but also separate provision for those over compulsory school age,
i.e. further education.

The 1988 Act has not essentially changed this aspect of provision, except in one major respect. Further education is now much
more closely defined, ensuring that 16–19 education (apart from
what continues in schools) is largely separate from what is now
called higher education. In this respect, LEAs will no longer have
the duty to secure provision of the latter (Section 120.1). On the
other hand they will, in addition to their duty to provide further
education in their own area, have the power to provide for those
living outside their area (Section 120.2). Although LEAs have in
fact been doing this for a good many years the Act clearly legiti-
mizes current (not necessarily legal) practice.

An important aspect of the 1988 Act, reflecting the market

approach to further education, is the delegation of financial and other managerial powers to the governing bodies of FE colleges (Sections 142 and 148). On the surface this may be construed as the elimination of local authority bureaucracy and the promotion of self-government. Colleges will apparently be able to be much more responsive to their own needs, having the powers to manage their finances in the way that they think fit and to hire and fire staff when necessary. In fact, the Act gives governing bodies the ability to delegate further their financial powers to college principals, a sub-section (142.6.b) which surely will not have gone unnoticed, or indeed unsupported, by college managements!

The manner in which these delegated powers are to be used by governing bodies may depend to some extent upon the membership of these bodies. Here, the Act points to a fundamental change: employers will now be in a more powerful position to decide the direction of further education since their representatives could take up at least half the places on the governing bodies of FE colleges (Section 152). At the same time no more than 20 per cent of the governing body members may be LEA appointees. The significance of this change should not be underestimated, especially given one of the dominant themes of this book that the role of local authorities in the control of education—and in other aspects of collective provision of services—has been seriously challenged.

Finally, it should be noted that Chapter 1 of the Act (The Curriculum), while dealing with schools, does give reserve powers to central government in relation to 16–19-year-olds whether at school or in FE colleges (Section 24). In Section 19 the Act also states that courses leading to external qualifications may have to be approved by the Secretary of State.

EFFECTS OF THE ACT

With local education authority control of public sector higher education having, in large measure, been stripped away, where is further education left? In theory, local education authorities retain the duty to secure provision of adequate further education. In practice the situation may be rather different. Whether or not they have made sufficient FE provision, LEAs will have decreasing responsibility for the education and training of 16–19-year-olds. Instead the fate of these people will be increasingly in the hands of employers, as managing agents for the Youth Training Scheme, and the Department of Employment, as a major purchaser (25 per cent) of further education courses and the sole funding authority for TVEI. Interestingly, it was reported (*Times Educational Supplement*, 29 July 1988) that the short-lived Training Commission feared that its control might be weakened by the 1988 Act as a result of the shift in power from LEAs to individual schools and colleges.

A further outcome of the separation of further from higher education is the effect upon the teaching force. On the surface this seems a logical move: a vertical division between different levels of learning manifested in different curricula and a different pattern of qualifications. This apparently assumes two distinct teaching forces with two distinct orientations to teaching. After all, it might be argued that universities are distinct from school sixth forms and one would not expect the two teaching forces here to overlap. Yet the situation is not as clear-cut as some would make out. Teachers in further education institutions vary considerably in the levels of work in which they are involved. Much has depended on the historical development of particular FE colleges. Many, it is true, have tended to concentrate on low-level work serving the vocational and academic needs of the 16–19 population almost exclusively. Other colleges, however, have evolved as mixed economy institutions undertaking work at diverse levels, from vocational preparation to postgraduate research. A number of these colleges developed as monotechnics where it was thought appropriate to concentrate a large number of courses relating to one vocational area (such as the London College of Printing and the London College of Furniture).

In such mixed economy colleges teachers have very often welcomed the breadth of work offered in the way of GCE, City and Guilds, B/TEC and CNAA degree courses. On the other hand, there are some who would clearly like to divest themselves of all non-advanced further education, particularly if it involves teaching less than willing students on YTS and similar vocationalist programmes. Pressures on local education authorities to split colleges into separate further and higher education institutions might well arise as a result, with the new HE colleges achieving independent status as corporate organizations funded through the Polytechnics and Colleges Funding Council. (In fact, this has already happened with, for example, the hiving-off of non-advanced FE work from Cambridgeshire College of Arts and Technology, so allowing it to enter the PCFC sector.) Many LEAs, in turn, will probably resist such pressure to avoid losing ownership and control of a substantial segment of post-compulsory education.

Essentially, further education colleges will be placed in the position of having to compete on an enlarged scale with schools for business from a declining 16–19 population (even though in amending the 1944 Act, full-time FE courses are not to be regarded as secondary education). Moreover, local education authorities may decide on a stricter separation of educational provision, with the location of academic general education courses (GCSE and A levels) being entirely within schools rather than FE colleges. Indeed, there is evidence that this had already happened before the Act in more than one LEA. While the intention may not necessarily be elitist, the consequence of attempting to protect schools from the effects of falling rolls (even if sixth form consortia are the order of the day) is the promotion and reinforcement of segregation of 16–19 education. It is a move that flies in the face of the tertiary college model, which arguably is the rational solution, even though it may require some kind of commitment to integration of provision and an end to educational stratification.

With the Department of Employment taking increasing responsibility for funding FE provision and the difficulties faced in the promotion of pre-vocational courses (such as CPVE) where the funding is from the LEA and where students receive no financial support the situation is even more serious. On top of this, colleges in the south are having to come to terms with increased job opportunities for young people. Whether or not this is merely a temporary phenomenon, a consequence of the late 1980s boom, there is bound to be tremendous pressure on college managements to devise survival strategies through the exploitation of different markets (such as special needs, short full-cost courses for industry, and so on).

On the other hand, FE colleges will continue to promote vocational programmes of all kinds, leading to a variety of craft and commercial qualifications (B/TEC, City and Guilds, RSA, etc.) that are to come under the umbrella of the National Council for Vocational Qualifications (NCVQ). This body, which will eventually accredit all vocational qualifications, places a clear emphasis on competence criteria for the award of such qualifications and, in so doing, stands in contrast to the objectives of the national curriculum, given its emphasis on a broad education. As a result, there may well be discontinuity between the FE curriculum and the secondary school curriculum. Whether this will be a case for the use of the reserve powers by the Secretary of State, as mentioned earlier, to bring the national curriculum into FE colleges (for 16–19-year-olds) remains to be seen.

All in all, the 1988 Act, in so far as it deals with the 16–19 population, merely adds a further dimension to a wider government policy which seeks to control the fortunes of the young. Vocationalism has meant that except for a minority most school-leavers will find that they have been ascribed a new status. They are no longer to be considered as entrants to the labour market but rather as recruits to vocational preparation. Whether or not the economic situation changes to allow more 16-year-olds to be employed straight from school, the general trend is such that the school–work transition is not seen as the natural progression that it used to be. Sixteen-year-olds can now expect to continue in a state of dependancy rather than achieve the relative independence that goes with employment.

With the new social security regulations in force there is now no way that school leavers can claim the status of employees unless in work. As from September 1988, except for those categorized as severely disabled or in some other special situation, social security payments (Income Support) will no longer be available for 16 and 17-year-olds. The 21 hour rule, whereby it was possible to engage in a course of study for up to 21 hours per week without losing entitlement to benefit, now becomes largely irrelevant if Income Support is not normally payable for this age group.

By design or as a consequence of other aspects of government policy, existing social divisions are likely to be reinforced as far as 16–19 education is concerned. Since the 21 hour rule enabled young people to study on an almost full-time basis and retain a degree of financial independence, the likelihood is that there will be an increased conscription to YTS schemes, leaving established FE courses as the preserve of those who are able to obtain financial support from parents. (In this respect, the implications for students with, say, moderate learning difficulties or moderate physical disabilities may be quite devastating.) Yet even here YTS is not without its difficulties, especially with regard to its operation in urban areas. Irregular attendance, premature departure and lack of employer involvement have all been seen as evidence of disenchantment with a scheme that all too often fails to fulfil its aims. A shortage of high quality work placements, under-representation of young people from ethnic minorities on employer-based schemes and continuing discrimination in the job market have highlighted the relative ineffectiveness of YTS in inner cities (*Financial Times*, 14 December 1987).

In conclusion, the 1988 Education Act has, to some degree, rationalized the post-compulsory public sector education scene. Further education is now distinct from higher education (although this appears to be little different from the old advanced/non-advanced divide). More importantly is the change in control of further education, especially when viewed within the context of the declining position of local government on the one hand and the increased centralized control of youth on the other. At long last, the age of incrementalism in further education policy-making seems to be over; after 100 years of what might be called 'expressed need and unsystematic effort' (Lawson & Silver, 1973, p.408) the central state decided to take command of the school–work transition process.

If this means real coherence in 16–19 education and training, with progression from compulsory schooling and genuine opportunities for career development or entry into higher education, then whatever comes out of the 1988 Act and other state initiatives will be welcomed. What concerns many teachers and young people is that much of this appears to constitute a superficial exercise only, since there is a failure to tackle underlying structural problems that give rise to disenchantment, lack of hope and social conflict. Some of these issues are taken up in a discussion of structural contradictions in Chapter 9.

REFERENCES

* Bash, L., Coulby, D. & Jones, C. (1985) *Urban Schooling: Theory and Practice*. London: Cassell.
* Cohen, P. (1986) (186) No kidding—it's a really useful knowledge? *Social Science Teacher*, vol.16, no.1.
* Dale, R. (1986) Examining the gift horse's teeth: a tentative analysis of TVEI. In Walker, S. & Barton, L. (eds), *Youth, Unemployment and Schooling*. Milton Keynes: Open University Press.
* Gleeson, D. (1983) Further education, tripartism and the labour market. In Gleeson, D. (ed.), *Youth Training and the Search for Work*. London: Routledge.
* Lawson, J. & Silver, H. (1973) *A Social History of Education in England*. London: Methuen.

6

The Break-up of the Inner London Education Authority

Crispin Jones

BACKGROUND

In a BBC *World at One* broadcast in early 1988, J.K. Galbraith, reflecting on Mrs Thatcher's government's predilection for using the word 'reform' in relation to its policies, commented: 'I would reserve the word reform for more socially progressive measures'. He went on to quote himself, reminding the interviewer of the comment he had made some 20 years ago in relation to what had happened to many of the cities in the United States, namely, that they were places where private affluence could bee seen alongside public squalor. The same division, he claimed, was increasingly visible in British cities, particularly in London, the British city with which he was most familiar. With the breaking up of the Inner London Education Authority (ILEA), there is a real danger of the educational component of London's 'public squalor' becoming even more apparent.

Given that the clauses in the Education Reform Act relating to the breaking up of the ILEA appear the most partisan ones, the question has to be asked as to why the ILEA, and its predecessors, the London County Council (LCC) and the London School Board, have continually caused problems for central government, particularly when that central authority has been Conservative controlled. This historical antagonism needs to be explored in more detail if the break-up of the ILEA is to be understood. If this is not done, there is a danger of a simplistic reading of current government policy towards education as embodied in the Education Reform Act. In other words, the break-up of the ILEA is not a sudden, partisan measure dreamt up by a vengeful Conservative administration and hastily cobbled on to the Education Reform Bill, although that is a partial explanation. It is more a historical conjunction of oppositional educational forces in a critical site, namely the capital city. This chapter, consequently, is based on a dual contention:

1. That the education system of London has often been seen as

the focus for oppositional pedagogic discourse and practice in relation to the discourse and practices espoused by the central government. Furthermore, the physical location of both parties within the capital exacerbates rather than diminishes this conflict.

2. That the political conflict inherent in most modern nation states between proponents of nationalism and the nation takes place in cities rather than the marginalized rural peripheries, and, central to this chapter, educational provision is a key element in such conflict.

These contentions are explored below, so that the final section, on the actual abolition of the ILEA, can be placed more centrally in the debate about the nature of schooling within the urban systems of capitalist nation states.

When the London School Board came into being, the aim of its originators was to bring about a more orderly and organized provision of education for the urban masses in Victorian London. Included in that concern for administrative order was a demand for a better educated and compliant urban work force. The inculcation of middle-class gender distinctions, a process well documented by Mica Nava (1984), was also important, the more so as it is still deeply influential in terms of attitudes towards the teaching of working-class girls. However, to assume that the provision of mass education was some sort of ideological subversion of the working-class is a *post hoc* oversimplification. There were philanthropic and libertarian strands running through the period of the London School Board, strands that were often oppositional to the views espoused by both central government and conservative elements within the Board itself.

From its outset the Board was a political battleground between these various parties. Seen by some as a potential arena for the liberation of working-class children in the traditional 'knowledge is power' mode, it was seen by others as a potentially revolutionary body engaged in subversion of the status quo if not of the state itself.

This struggle is best illustrated by the debates over the Cockerton Judgment of 1899. This judgment forbade the *de facto* secondary education that the Board had been providing for high attaining working-class children. Because the 1870 Act did not really visualize more than a basic elementary education for the urban masses, this extension of education introduced by the London Board, meritocratic as it might seem today, was seen in a different light by many at the time. The legal case, initiated by the Board's auditor (in itself an interesting precursive action), was decided against the Board. Not only was the practice declared illegal but the disquiet felt over the activities of the London School Board in this and other instances was very much at the front of the minds of those who drafted the 1902 Education Act. This Act, among other things, abolished the London School Board, education in London being put under the control of the new body, the London County Council. This body, responsible for a whole range of urban services in the capital, was thought to be a more effective and less disturbing way of running London's education

In many ways, this was so. If inner London's schools can be said to have had a golden age, it was during the LCC period, at least on the surface. For example, to teach in an LCC school was seen as prestigious and, for quite long periods of time, teaching posts in the LCC were difficult to get because of the competition for them. This was particularly the case for newly qualified teachers, who had to have first-rate final grades if they were to be even considered by the LCC.

This rosy picture is only a partial view, as it sees London's education as divorced from the national economic context within which it prospered. The reality was that, for much of the inter-war period, socioeconomic conditions in London were *generally* better than in many other urban areas in Britain. This is not asserting much, for conditions of life remained grim in many working-class areas of London, such as Bermondsey and Stepney. Nor did the Second World War and the post-war redevelopment greatly improve matters, as the work of the Institute of Community Studies reveals (Young & Willmott, 1962; Madge & Willmot, 1981).

Despite the LCC's educational success, its educational work ended in 1965 with the abolition of the LCC and the creation of the Greater London Council. The political motivation for abolition was not primarily educational but was more global. Among other things, it was hoped that the incorporation into a new all-London body of leafy and traditionally conservative suburban boroughs, such as Bexley, Kingston, Barnet and Bromley, would end the Labour Party's near-monopoly of power over the capital's business. The position on education was more ambiguous. The suburbs valued their education (many were already virtually autonomous) and would not accept a London-wide authority; equally, most of the new inner London boroughs did not want it either, fearing the imposition of educational policies with which they did not agree. Subsequently, the Inner London Education Authority was established as a permanent, quasi-autonomous committee of the GLC, responsible for education in the old LCC area. More clearly than ever before, the education of the poor of London appeared to have been split from the education of the better-off.

That is not to say that all the children in the ILEA were poor, or that all of London's poor children were in the ILEA. Outer London boroughs like Newham and Haringey had areas of severe deprivation, while the western ILEA boroughs, such as Hammersmith and Fulham, had areas of extreme wealth. Even the boroughs in the East had areas of neighbourhood revitalization or gentrification where the new professional middle-classes, rejecting the suburbia of their own childhood as well as appreciating the economic advantage they could take of an inner city location, moved back into areas deserted by their nineteenth-century predecessors. Many of this group of incomers were politically active and sent their own children to state schools. They quickly became a powerful force in inner London politics, including the government of the ILEA.

The first obvious public signs of the tensions that this could lead to were revealed in the William Tyndale 'affair' in 1975. The ILEA's own enquiry (ILEA, 1977) revealed a sorry catalogue of factionalism and incompetence. In a small inner city primary school in Islington, perhaps the most famous area for gentrification, the conflicting educational expectations of parents, teachers and politicians had all but destroyed the school. The media coverage of the affair brought into public prominence for the first time the idea of the so-called 'loony left' teacher. Furthermore, the publication of the report helped establish a political climate that led to Prime Minister Callaghan's Ruskin speech and the start of the anything-but-Great Debate. One element of this debate was that it revealed a loss of confidence in city education by elements in the Labour Party. Finally, the subsequent general election returned a Conservative government led by a former Minister of Education who had, for a variety of reasons, no love for the ILEA.

The crisis in confidence in the ILEA was momentarily halted during the early tenure of office of Peter Newsam as Education Officer. The Marshall Report (GLC, 1978) confirmed the value of a unitary education authority for inner London and the 1980 HMI report on ILEA was generally favourable concluding:

> The picture that currently emerges is of a caring and generous authority with considerable analytical powers to identify problems, the scale of which is, in some cases, unique in this country.... Performance in nursery and primary education and in further and higher education is generally sound and improving. In secondary schools and special education per-

formance is much patchier; it calls for the same kind of firm handling which has improved the other sectors.

(DES, 1980, section 21.16)

The improvement of existing practice and new initiatives in areas such as multi-ethnic education seemed to indicate that the lessons of the Tyndale affair had been learnt and that the Authority was regaining its pre-eminence within LEAs in Britain.

However, as the Conservative government became more firmly established, winning a further general election and pushing through a range of major legislation affecting many aspects of society, the ILEA became increasingly the focus for a view of education seemingly at odds with the government. Sir Keith Joseph, the Secretary of State, was very concerned with certain aspects of ILEA policy and would have liked to have abolished it at the same time as the GLC was abolished in 1985. (Technically, as a committee of the GLC it should have shared that body's fate.) However, much of the advice he received was in favour of its retention, and he was persuaded to retain it, making it, under the 1985 Local Government Act, a directly elected education authority, the first of its kind in the United Kingdom.

The new form of mandate that direct elections gave the ILEA did not really appease the central government, who increasingly saw the educational activities of left-wing LEAs like the ILEA as directly oppositional to their own policies, which indeed they often were. Their concern was taken up by the popular press, which ran what in retrospect seems like an oppositional campaign to the work of many of these councils, particularly in the area of equal educational opportunities.

Although the issue of class inequality would appear to be the core issue around which such arguments would pivot, it was in fact policies to do with education and racial equality that caused the greatest concern. There are several reasons for this. The first is that the ILEA, like other left-wing education authorities, preferred, in policy terms at least, to make racial inequality a priority over class inequality. Why this was so is a most interesting question, having more to do with the apparent intractability of the issue of class and education than with people considering it unimportant. A second reason is that issues relating to sexual and gender equality, although no less controversial, had been on the educational agenda for a shorter period of time. A consequence of this focus was that core values of the British nation state were challenged, a most worrying state of affairs to those who had a vision of a monolithic unitary British nation state and were fearful of its putative common values being 'swamped'. The abolition of the ILEA was, in retrospect, a clear response to the bringing to the fore of the national question in the capital city, on the doorstep of the nation state's government, a point that will now be developed.

The Education Reform Act applies only to two nations within the British state, namely England and Wales. Yet there is little in the Act which recognizes that Wales might have educational priorities and aspirations different from those of England. A nod towards the Welsh language is there, almost grudgingly, and that is that. The establishment of a Welsh Curriculum Council can be seen as either regulatory of a curriculum, the parameters of which have been set in England, or as a way in which the curriculum of Welsh schools can sustain and develop Welsh culture within a British context. Your view on this is most likely to be shaped by the side of the border you are standing on. At one level, the issue of Wales and the Welsh shows that part of the motivation for the Education Reform Act, and in particular those clauses relating to the abolition of the ILEA, reflects a curious and dangerous recurring fear of the English right, namely the fear of being overrun by the non-English British, with the consequent break-up of the English-led British nation state.

In our cities, and particularly in London, groups of British people who are discriminated against in all sorts of ways, even to the point of being physically attacked, are seen as a threat to the English sense of being the 'owners' of Britain. Groups of Afro-Caribbean British, Muslim British and Turkish-speaking British are seen by far too many English people as in some strange way threatening the cultural integrity not of the English, but of the British nation, the two having long been conflated in their heads. Thus when the ILEA took seriously the implications of this national pluralism within the British state in terms of its consequences for education, this was seen as being of a different order of challenge to the status quo from other ILEA initiatives in relation to class, gender and special educational needs.

At this point it is useful to make a distinction between anti-racism and pluralism and between the concerns of the British nation state and many members of its black population. This is because there is agreement, at the level of public rhetoric at least, that racist practices are evil and should be challenged. However, pluralism is potentially threatening to the stability of the state and racism can thus be partly seen as a set of practices that sustain singularity and reject pluralism. Plurality of languages, religions, political practice, economic arrangements, cultural and family structures pose threatening questions to the stability of the nation state. However, in the British context, the plurality of physical appearance arouses the deepest atavistic fears in both individual English people and more significantly within the institutions of an English-dominated nation state.

Objections to the ILEA's anti-racist/multi-ethnic educational initiative, although seemingly focused on its anti-racist strategies, were also objections to the idea of religious, linguistic and other forms of pluralism. And as that diversity was so significant in range and quantity in London, those educational practices that appeared to recognize such plurality were seen as deeply threatening. This is not a new phenomenon: British history is full of episodes where plurality was suppressed. The marginalized position of Catholics in Britain has a long history and to this day is perceived as legitimate in certain parts of Britain. The same is true of British Jews and also of the other languages of Britain, Anti-semitism is still a subtle undercurrent in British society, while Welsh and Gaelic were only comparatively recently allowed into the school curriculum.

In pragmatic terms it was the manifestation of diversity within the primate city, London, which, as in previous decades, challenged both the unitary conception of the nation state and the ideological support to this concept that was enshrined in its institutions, including education. And it was pluralistic local responses to this that set off almost a moral panic within those groups who saw the unity of the nation state being threatened.

From this it may be claimed that the issue is not so much why the ILEA was abolished but why abolition took so long. Part of the answer to that perhaps lies in the substitution of Kenneth Baker for Sir Keith Joseph as Secretary of State for Education. It could be said that the substitution was one of action for thought. Joseph at least was aware of the complexity of issues that such policies raised for a national education system; it is doubtful if Baker was. Certainly his public pronouncements on the issue reveal little on the subject, although his poetic preferences are more revealing.

Within the context of a nation-state-enhancing Education Act, with its national(ist) curriculum and enhanced central control of whole swathes of education, the abolition of the ILEA becomes an event of considerable symbolic importance rather than the political settling of old scores. It reaffirms the determination of the nation state to retain its position as the sole arbiter of what it is to be British. It also demonstrates that, as has often been the case in the past, it is education in the large cities that has challenged this assertion.

THE TERMS OF THE ACT AND THEIR CONSEQUENCES

On April 1, 1990 the following shall cease to exist—
  (a) the Inner London Education Authority (in this part
      referred to as 'ILEA') and any education committee
      established by that authority; and
  (b) the Inner London Education Area.

(Education Reform Act, 1988, section 3.1)

The abolition of the ILEA does little to abolish the material conditions within which it operates. Comparisons with other cities only serve to emphasize the unique educational environment found in inner London, for 'there is greater deprivation in Inner London than in Birmingham, Liverpool or Manchester' (ILEA, 1984, p.7).

Boroughs like Hackney and Lambeth precariously hover on the edge of viability, irrespective of the political complexion of their elected members. Paul Harrison's account of Hackney (Harrison, 1983) makes it very clear that the so-called affluent south-east has passed by Hackney. He sees it, in a telling analogy, as the third world transposed into the first, competition at the bottom of the global heap. On the major social indices of deprivation, Hackney, like several other inner London local authorities, is always near the 'top' of the national lists. Thus there are unusually high levels of unemployment and infant mortality, large numbers of overcrowded households often lacking basic amenities, old people living alone and rapid demographic changes. Many of the single parent families are very poor, and too many are still stranded in disastrous tower blocks or poor-quality short-stay council accommodation. Furthermore, for black people living in inner London, economic disadvantage is increased by racism, prejudice and discrimination. A Parliamentary Select Committee noted on the Bangladeshi population in Tower Hamlets:

69 per cent of Bangladeshis were unskilled or semi-skilled manual workers, compared with 43 per cent of Pakistanis, 35 per cent of West Indians and 16 per cent of white people. Many of course are unemployed. Lack of skills is reflected in earnings: in 1984 median weekly pay for Bangladeshi men was £88.50, the next lowest earnings for Asian men being £106.20 among Pakistanis.

(Home Affairs Committee, 1987, para.14.)

There is a danger in such catalogues of gloom that the ability of the people concerned to act as more than passive victims of an uncaring society is overlooked. Harrison's account of Hackney, for example, is flawed by such a deficit model of Hackney's poorest inhabitants. To survive these material conditions requires a depth and strength of character that one would be hard pressed to find in the leafy and prosperous suburbs. To ignore is easy, to survive the consequences of such ignorance is not.

Thus education in such an environment is always going to be difficult. A report on changes in the education priority index produced by ILEA in 1985 noted that:

> One in four primary schoolchildren in inner London has both parents unemployed, and in some parts of the city, the figure rises to one in two. Nearly half of inner London's primary schoolchildren are entitled to free school meals. The measures of poverty ... show a level of deprivation which is completely unacceptable in our capital city.

> (ILEA, 1985, p.iii)

To place these figures in their national context, the free meals figure, for example, is over twice the national average; moreover, the report showed a worsening trend since the index had last been analysed in 1983. In other words, the increasing prosperity in the south-east of England had passed by many of the parents of ILEA's children.

Because of the history of conflict with central government over educational policy and practice, it is not surprising that the Education Reform Bill proposed the abolition of the ILEA. Rate capping had failed to bring the authority to financial or ideological heel, and the directly elected authority was of the same outlook as the former authority. When the Bill was published, it was clear that the ILEA had a real fight on its hands if it was to survive this latest attack on its existence. The widespread approval of new proposals for secondary education put forward by the Hargreaves Report (ILEA, 1984) had faded away, as their implementation proved difficult, particularly with widespread disruption being caused in schools by the teachers' pay dispute. This latter activity had inevitably alienated a considerable number of parents, a group of great significance in beating off earlier forays against the ILEA.

Perhaps most significant was the fact that the abolition of the ILEA was but one part of a massive piece of educational legislation which had many other controversial aspects to it. As a consequence, much of the early debate about the ILEA was quite low key. Thus a generally favourable HMI paper on the ILEA by the Chief Inspector, Eric Bolton, was duly leaked to the press but gave little ammunition to either party, being little more than an update of the earlier 1980 report. A parents' poll came out in favour of the retention of the ILEA, which surprised few people and persuaded even fewer to change their minds on the issue. It confirmed earlier polls that showed parents, for quite sensible reasons, being unhappy about major upheavals in their children's education. Perhaps more significantly, reasoned arguments for the ILEA's continued existence, as found in the Authority's response (ILEA, 1987) to the DES consultation paper *The Organisation of Education in Inner London* (DES, 1987) went almost unnoticed. Indeed, the questions raised in that response paper still largely remain unanswered, the government too often exploiting a very large parliamentary majority that did not particularly want to hear arguments about the merits of the ILEA's abolition.

If there was concern in Parliament, it was primarily about the mechanics of abolition and the consequences for the voluntary-aided schools in London of the opting-out clauses elsewhere in the Bill. On the former, an unlikely combination of Norman Tebbit and Michael Heseltine, two former Conservative ministers, forced through an amendment that abolished the ILEA outright rather than allowing for a more drawn-out end. It also prevented the formation of a rump ILEA which would have represented many of the oppositional characteristics that the abolition of the ILEA was meant to do away with. The concern for opting out meant that much of the energy that could have been used for the defence of the ILEA was spent on preserving the authority of the Churches in relation to the schooling that they provided. As this defence was spearheaded by the Bishop of London, it meant that more general concerns for the ILEA took somewhat of a back seat.

When key officers in the Authority took on new posts elsewhere, particularly the Education Officer, William Stubbs, and the Chief Inspector, David Hargreaves, a feeling quite quickly arose that this time the Authority would go. The political battle was handled badly, with inept remarks about inevitable success (or failure) being made before critical debates on the subject. Finally, because the abolition was only part of the Bill, opposition was divided in its concerns and at no time was a really vigorous lobby built up for the ILEA, despite worthy efforts by Jack Straw, the Labour education spokesperson, and a handful of other opposition MPs and peers.

As the Bill went through Parliament, accumulating amendments as a sailing ship does barnacles, the changes to the sections on the abolition of the ILEA were minor. There was one of some importance, giving the Secretary of State powers of vetting senior appointments in the new London LEAs, but at the time of writing, with many of those appointments having been made, there is little evidence of the power being used. It was a curious point, however, and revealed the levels of paranoia among some sections within central government, as well as being a fine example of the 'I must imprison you so that you may be free' school of libertarian thought in the Thatcherite wing of the Conservative Party.

On completion of the Bill's passage through Parliament, the government announced further rate capping measures against the authority, presumably to ensure that expenditure is brought down before abolition, thus lowering the cost of the financial 'cushion' that the government is providing for an interim period after abolition to maintain some measure of financial continuity and stability. However, the current cuts will reduce both the ILEA's and the successor boroughs' financial options. In cash terms it has meant cuts in real terms of 10 per cent for the financial year 1988/9 and 8 per cent for the year 1989/90 (ILEA, 1988a). The poll tax will adversely affect boroughs with a low adult:child ratio, like Tower Hamlets, because it will produce far less money per *child* than in boroughs with a high ratio. Thus disadvantaged boroughs will not only start off with a parlous financial position but will see that position getting worse as the new tax is introduced.

A further point that arises from this new tax in relation to some of the inner London boroughs is that their demographic profiles may make its implementation fall foul of Section 1(1)(b) of the 1976 Race Relations Act, which defines and makes illegal indirect discrimination, i.e. acts which by their *consequences* rather than their *intentions* discriminate against racial groups. This potential illegality arises from the demographic fact that newly arrived minority groups usually contain more people of child-producing age and during the initial phase of settlement produce larger families. Thus, in a borough like Tower Hamlets, with an increasing child population among its racial minority groups, the new poll tax will further disadvantage groups who are already severely disadvantaged.

Even if this is not grounds for potential litigation, the financial stringency will affect the poorer LEAs especially badly, given the nature of the educational issues that they face. To demonstrate this, the key issues that face Tower Hamlets deserve closer examination, for although they are not typical in detail, many of the other new LEAs will face a similar scale of problem.

In Tower Hamlets, a dominating issue is the provision of effective education for the ethnic minority communities, particularly the Bangladeshi community. Specifically, the group has continuing and growing needs for English language teaching. As the ILEA's own comment on its statistics says:

> The Bengali speaking PHLOEs [pupils with home language other than English] had the lowest proportion of speakers who were fluent in English. This was also the case in 1985 and 1983. But more worryingly still the population of Bengali speakers fluent in English had steadily decreased with successive censuses from 17% in 1981 to 10% in 1987. ILEA provides no explanation for this adverse trend.

(ILEA, 1988b, p.2)

Thus the ILEA acknowledges that the language issue in Tower Hamlets appears intractable despite the effort that has been put into it. Yet a new LEA, with a complete education service to provide from scratch, is being expected to tackle this major issue, very probably with fewer resources than the ILEA had. This is not to argue that greater resources automatically lead to greater efficiency but that fewer resources are less likely to.

The position over effective language provision is only one of the major educational problems that will face the new authorities. Although statutory provision will continue, much of the non-statutory provision that ILEA saw as essential if it was to meet adequately the educational needs of inner London is now under threat. The consequences of its loss may well be unforeseen. Adult education, for example, as well as exemplifying the concept of life-long education with which few would disagree, offers, in the particular context of inner London, a real lifeline to many groups of people. This does not just mean young people, who are often seen as the more traditional inner city clients of adult education, but also the old, for whom adult education classes are crucial in terms of their getting out, meeting people and, ultimately, helping to ensure their continued vitality.

There are other areas like this, not all of them non-statutory. The careers service is to be organized on a London-wide basis but only because there were real fears that abolition would ensure its fragmentation. School meals, youth provision and nursery education are also potentially under threat and special educational provision is going to be very difficult to organize effectively. Major curriculum initiatives and the drive for equal opportunities in education are likely to fall victim to the break-up, although some boroughs will attempt to continue with them. The nationally acclaimed work of the ILEA's Research and Statistics Branch is also likely to be discontinued, even if the boroughs do work out some form of co-operation over the collection of statistics.

More difficult to tie down is the real sense of loss that many ILEA employees will feel on becoming a small LEA employee. ILEA teachers, for example, thought of themselves as all-London teachers without a strong divisional tie. No doubt this will change but it will change slowly. There is also the feeling among some ILEA teachers that by its division, the inner London teaching force will become more amenable to both management and the national teachers' unions, some of the latter having found their ILEA members difficult to control in the past. The teachers in schools, however, are at least assured of a job after abolition. Many other, non-school-based, staff are not so lucky and will have to apply for new jobs in the new LEAs, with no guarantee of employment.

The consequences of other parts of the Act for those who work in the new-style inner London boroughs must be recognized. The imposition of city technology colleges will have a negative effect on the general quality of city schools, as will the opting-out provisions. All-black ghetto schools, with poor facilities and standards, may well become a reality with the government's implicit approval. Poorly resourced working-class schools will certainly come into being. However, linguistic and religious minorities may wish to establish schools and opt in, posing interesting questions for the Secretary of State, who has to give approval. Given the conservatism of many of the supporters of such forms of education, it is likely that permission will be given. However, will the views of the children concerned be taken into much consideration? Last but not least, the new national curriculum seems likely to ignore much of the cultural, linguistic and religious diversity that has been such an exciting aspect of London's education over the past 20 years or so. It is more likely to be a nationalist than a national curriculum, and the testing procedures will reinforce this unless the test designers are very careful indeed.

All should not be seen as doom and gloom. After the devastation, the schoolchildren will be the same, and many of the issues and many of the conflicts will be the same. The abolition of the ILEA merely moves legitimate educational discontent and innovation from County Hall to the town halls of inner London. Positive moves that have been generally admired, such as the innovatory work in linking schools with employers, will remain even though the government, as for example over the working of the Boston Compact in Hackney and Tower Hamlets, has been at some pains to try to assert that such practice scarcely exists, or if it does, it is not in the ILEA.

At a more abstract level, the place of pluralism within the British state remains to be resolved and London's education system, however administered, will continue to be a focus for discussion and action on this matter. In a similar way, oppositional educational practice will continue in the new London LEAs, albeit on a diminished scale, while the full effects of abolition are worked through. In other words, the educational issues that the ILEA posed for the state cannot, unlike the ILEA, be legislated away. Consequently, the next decade has the potential for being one of the most exciting ones in the history of London education, providing that the financial cuts do not bite so deeply that they destroy the service. The abolition of the ILEA refocuses our attention and provides a new starting point in the struggle for the democratization of education and, it is hoped, of the wider society.

REFERENCES

• DES (1980) *Report by HM Inspectors on Educational Provision by the Inner London Education Authority*. London: DES.
• DES (1987) *The Organisation of Education in Inner London*. London: DES.
• GLC (1978) *Inquiry on Greater London (The Marshall Report)*. London: GLC.
• Harrison, P. (1983) *Inside the Inner City*. Harmondsworth: Penguin.
• Home Affairs Committee (1987) *Bangladeshis in Britain*. Session 1986-87; First Report, 96–1. London: HMSO.
• ILEA (1977) *The William Tyndale School Public Inquiry (The Auld Report)*. London: ILEA.
• ILEA (1984) *Improving Secondary Schools (The Hargreaves Report)*. London: ILEA.
• ILEA (1985) *Children in Need: The Growing Needs of Inner London Schoolchildren*, RS 994/85. London: ILEA.
• ILEA (1987) *Authority Response to 'the Organisation of Education in Inner London'*. London: ILEA.
• ILEA (1988a) *ILEA News, no.54*. London: ILEA.
• ILEA (1988b) *Report on: ILEA Research and Statistics Branch Language Census 1987*. Unpublished paper. London: ILEA.
• Madge, C. & Willmott, P. (1981) *Inner City Poverty in Paris and London*. London: Routledge.

- Nava, M. (1984) The urban, the domestic and education for girls. In Grace, G. (ed.), *Education and the City*. London: Routledge.
- Young, M. & Willmott, P. (1962) *Family and Kinship in East London*. Harmondsworth: Penguin.

7

Higher Education and the Enterprise Culture

David Coulby

THE BACKGROUND

Chapter 4 emphasized the way in which the new national curriculum for schools is still dominated by traditional, academicist knowledge. At the higher education level, however, tradition in terms of both knowledge and processes has come under a challenge from the three successive Thatcher administrations. The 1988 Act is only the most recent culmination of these challenges. Before this the whole of higher education had been opened up to scrutiny by the exponents of the market economy and the enterprise culture. The values traditionally associated with higher education—excellence, imagination, research, creativity, experiment, culture, etc.—were not accepted at their face value in the course of this scrutiny. Instead new criteria of cost-effectiveness, standards and enterprise were introduced.

During the financial cuts of the early 1980s the University Grant Committee (UGC) made a key decision not to diminish the unit of resource. This meant they would not take more students for the same amount of money, nor take additional students at a lower level of funding than had been previous practice. In this way they sought to protect group size, teaching time and library and laboratory facilities for the universities. The polytechnics and colleges, funded by the National Advisory Body (NAB), which had been established in 1982 at a time when the government had provisionally accepted that these institutions should remain in local government control, were both more vulnerable to political pressure and more flexible in their modes and styles of teaching. They continued to recruit more students, even though their unit of resource was eroded. The large polytechnics, with their forceful leadership and their expansionist policies, became the preferred model for the advocates of the values of efficiency and enterprise. Throughout the mid-1980s the NAB-funded sector of higher education increased its proportion of student numbers against the universities. Nevertheless, the universities retained their preferential funding, which allowed them to maintain more lavish facilities and to provide substantially more research time for their staff. The polytechnics began to question this binary divide in resource allocation.

Until the 1988 Act the majority of NAB-funded higher education institutions were under the control of LEAs; they were within the public sector. In some cases these were the LEAs that were the subject of the 'loony left' campaign described in Chapter 1. The Polytechnic of North London (PNL), controlled by the ILEA, became the *cause célèbre* of higher education in the mid-1980s. A damaging HMI report on its sociology department was amplified by press and politicians into an attack on both the institution and the subject. A student, Patrick Harrington, announced that he was a member of the National Front. When large-scale student protest followed, academic staff at PNL were asked to identify demonstrators from police photographs. Their refusal led to a High Court case and events at PNL became a daily component of the media output. When the case against the lecturers was ultimately dismissed PNL disappeared from the front pages. However, the publicity helped to consolidate traditional, elitist attitudes, which perceived colleges and polytechnics as the secondary moderns of higher education.

The dissatisfactions provoked by events at PNL confirmed more enduring reservations about non-university higher education. As Peter Scott notes:

> Nor should the institutional resilience and higher morale of the public sector conceal the fact that they are still caught up in a web of elitist assumptions, a hierarchy of assumed merit that ultimately favours the universities.

(Scott, 1988, pp.140–1)

These dissatisfactions were ultimately to focus not on the polytechnics themselves but rather on the LEAs and the Council for National Academic Awards (CNAA). If CNAA had validated the PNL sociology courses then were not its own procedures and personnel open to suspicion? CNNA's inexhaustible appetite for paperwork had become almost as legendary as the combative and negative style adopted by some of its panels when they visited institutions. For the larger and longer established institutions, CNAA had become something of an unnecessary burden. A Committee of Enquiry was set up and the subsequent *Lindop Report* was published in 1985 (Committee of Enquiry into the Academic Validation of Degree Courses in Public Sector Higher Education, 1985). As well as exposing the costly and bureaucratic nature of CNAA's procedures, this report was able to emphasize the maturity of many of the NAB-funded institutions and their ability to maintain the greater academic independence that they sought. CNAA was subsequently rapidly streamlined and the larger NAB-funded institutions began to be accredited for validating and monitoring their own degrees and other courses. (This has had the side-effect of leaving the smaller institutions as the only main concern of CNAA, thereby exposing them to an even greater degree of superfluous scrutiny.) The process of accreditation had given yet more independence and power to the polytechnics, many of which were finding LEA control increasingly constricting and irksome.

Institutional control was raised as an alternative to leaving the rapidly developing polytechnics in the hands of LEAs perceived as potentially wayward, even though such a change might leave them more vulnerable to central government intervention. Pressure in this direction came from the directors of polytechnics, ably orchestrated through the Committee of Directors of Polytechnics (CDP). LEA control over heads of budget, staffing establishment and capital allocation was seen as unnecessary and time-consuming interference. The difficulties varied according to the LEA in control, but many members of the CDP complained that their planning and enterprise were being stifled by unimaginative, uninformed town hall bureaucracy.

The UGC decision of 1981 to control the unit of resource had not shielded universities from the general cuts in the resourcing of public services that characterized the 1980s. In the name of efficiency and cost-effectiveness the UGC was reluctantly brought to accept the league tables that ranked them according to their research output. Scott comments:

> The Committee's controversial decision to grade the quality of the research in every university department, cloaked the much more significant drive towards cost-effectiveness, which in practice and of necessity has been interpreted as levelling down to the lowest defensible cost base.... Cost not quality has been the decisive factor in shaping the university system under the intolerable pressure of Tory austerity.

> (Scott, 1988, pp.139–40).

Accepting the impetus towards cost-effectiveness, the UGC itself initiated a steering committee on efficiency, which resulted in 1985 in the publication of *The Jarratt Report* (Committee of Vice-Chancellors and Principals, 1985). This indicated that one of the main obstacles to 'efficiency' in universities was the practice of tenure, whereby academics were given jobs for life and so could not be made redundant even if they no longer fulfilled an important teaching or research role. Secretary of State Joseph had attempted to persuade universities to abandon tenure, but with little success. The cause was taken up by his successor Kenneth Baker.

In each case the tenure issue was one of the more visible aspects of dissatisfaction with the universities. They were seen as being somehow out of the nation's control and as failing to co-operate as actively as they might in the economic revival that Thatcher's ministers saw themselves as pioneering. Hugo Young noted:

> Much more insistent is their [ministers'] reiterated assertion linking universities with the gross national product. The economic test, the business imperative, the contribution to British recovery, these are what matter.

> (Young, 1987)

Certainly, in terms of flexibility and cost-effectiveness, the universities were often seen to compare unfavourably with the growing polytechnics.

While the polytechnics quite readily accepted that they were competing against the universities and each other to obtain student numbers on courses, the universities were less ready to engage in the language and practices of the marketplace. With the size of the age cohort set to reduce rapidly in the late 1980s this may not have been a wise course. Their remoteness was seen as something which needed, in the national interest, to be remedied. While the polytechnics had moved towards central control almost by volition, the universities seemed to be doing so by default.

An initial impetus in the direction of the centralization of higher education came with DES Circular 3/84, whereby the Secretary of State (Joseph, at that time) took rigid control of teacher education. Before higher education institutions were endorsed for training teachers, they had to be satisfactorily inspected by HMI and subjected to scrutiny by the Council for the Accreditation of Teachers (CATE), which implemented the criteria centrally set down in 3/84. This brought all institutions that educate teachers into the close purview of the Secretary of State. In particular, it provided HMI with their first foothold into inspecting universities. University departments of education had to be inspected before receiving CATE approval. Although a polite fiction was maintained that HMI were there 'by invitation', many of the results of their scrutiny provided evidence for those who wished to cast doubt on the idea that the university sector achieved higher standards.

THE TERMS OF THE ACT

The Act deals with further and higher education together in Part
2. Further education is discussed in Chapter 6 above. The sections
of the Bill dealing with higher education (Sections 121–138) were
much amended during its progress through Parliament, particularly in the Lords. Where the ILEA and home economics could find
few friends, the vice-chancellors proved capable of marshalling
support in an attempt to diminish the amount of central control to
be applied both to themselves and to the newly free-standing
polytechnics and colleges.

Polytechnics and the larger higher education colleges and insti-
tutes are removed from LEA control. The 48 polytechnics and
colleges which had more than 55 per cent of their students on
higher education courses and more than 350 students in all are
incorporated as free-standing statutory corporations (Sections
121–128). This figure will rise to slightly more than 48 as other
institutions shed some of their non-advanced work in an attempt to
gain independence. The institutions are now controlled by their
own boards of governors. At least half the new governors must be
experienced in industry, business, commerce or the professions.
The numbers of academic staff and students eligible to become
governors are significantly reduced. Similarly, LEA representation on the new governing bodies is severely restricted. The staff,
buildings and property of the institutions passed from LEA ownership and control to that of the new independent corporations.
Funding of the higher education institutions is from central
government through a new body, the Polytechnics and Colleges
Funding Council (PCFC). The NAB is abolished (Sections 131 and
136).

The University Grant Committee is also abolished and replaced
by the University Funding Council (UFC) (Section 131). Like the
PCFC, this body is to consist of 15 people, all of whom are
appointed by the Secretary of State, and only nine of whom are to
come from higher education. Despite amendments in the Lords,
these two councils will have great powers and will be able to
specify, if they so wish, firm conditions to be followed if grants to
colleges, polytechnics and universities are to be made. However,
before they impose any such terms or conditions the councils are
required to consult with any institution concerned and with appropriate bodies, such as the Committee of Vice-Chancellors and Principals (CVCP) and CDP. The funding of higher education in
England and Wales is now almost exclusively central, placing
great power in the hands of the Secretary of State.

Tenure for academic staff in universities is abolished (Sections

202–208). New contracts which exclude the possibility of redundancy will be ruled as void. A Lords amendment attempted to ensure academic freedom by insisting that academics cannot be sacked on the basis of their opinions.

THE EFFECTS OF THE ACT

There is no doubt that the colleges and polytechnics will welcome and possibly benefit from freedom from LEA control and constraints. While the Bill was still before Parliament the CDP surprised many LEAs by welcoming the proposals. The large, mature institutions—most of them already effectively free of CNAA—will now have the autonomy they need to develop, expand and innovate. The competition they exert on the university sector is likely to become increasingly fierce. The economies of scale open to polytechnics, and their advantages as accredited institutions, will also make them strong competitors with the smaller independent colleges. A further round of amalgamations began when the Bill was still before Parliament. This, with its associated effects of destabilization, is likely to continue.

Not all the effects of the Act will be so beneficial, even for the polytechnics. The LEAs quickly withdrew their support for the institutions once the plans were announced. Between this announcement and vesting day (the point when the institutions formally achieved independence) on 1 April 1989, there was almost two years of planning blight when neither the LEAs nor central government were prepared to finance building programmes or capital allocation. Furthermore, many LEAs had supplied money additional to the NAB settlement to the institutions in their control. This subvention or top-up could amount to as much as several million pounds a year. Under the new regulations there is no possibility that such subventions will be available. Indeed LEAs took steps rapidly to eliminate these subventions as soon as the proposals were announced. They were expedited in this by the threat of rate-capping or, in the case of the ILEA, by the budget cut administered by central government. As well as contributing to the planning blight and providing institutions with short-term crises, these subvention eliminations have meant that important aspects of provision have, in some cases, been lost. It is easiest for higher education institutions to cut non-course-related provision: access developments, research programmes, library and computing budgets are among the areas that have suffered. The already relatively weak research base of the colleges and polytechnics has been further eroded.

The loss of links with the LEAs may have further and

enduringly deleterious effects on the colleges and polytechnics. The close links with LEAs facilitated the ability of public sector institutions to respond rapidly to expressed local needs. The development of part-time and mixed-mode courses, modular degrees and access courses have all been largely within the public sector. Local people with families and/or jobs, mature students returning to education, local professional, commercial and trade groups seeking technical and academic assistance could all find their needs flexibly catered for by the less rigid structures and processes developed within the public sector. Links between the institutions and schools and FE colleges have been developed and substantiated under the joint regulation of the LEAs. Similarly firm reciprocal links have been established with local industry and commerce and with cultural, social and administrative bodies. The institutions became attractive because of their many ties to the community and their responsiveness to local concerns. Obviously these local developments are unlikely to stop now that the institutions are autonomous. However, it is possible that the innovatory impulsion and the local support, which were the daily experience of the old arrangements, will gradually be diminished. The flexibility of the polytechnics and colleges to respond to new local needs and initiatives may be reduced.

The composition of the new governing bodies has given rise to misgivings among many in colleges and polytechnics. Student and academic membership is to be reduced and predominance given to business people. Brian Simon comments:

> This whole set of proposals has as its aim the transformation of the whole field of further education, including not only polytechnics and colleges of higher education, but also music, drama and art colleges—even adult education centres and colleges focussing largely on initial teacher training—into direct adjuncts of the local business world, having a solely utilitarian or instrumental direction.

(Simon, 1988, pp.98–9)

Local education authority governors, whatever their faults, did have a constituency within the local electorate. The Secretary of State employed management consultants to advise him on the acceptability of the people nominated to serve on the groups that would establish the new boards of governors for each institution. The only constituency to which the business representatives on these bodies can appeal is their acceptability to the Secretary of State. Apart from the non-democratic and centralist nature of these new bodies, there is no guarantee that they will have adequate knowledge of or sympathy with the academic activities of the institutions.

The 1988 Act signally failed to address the issue of the binary divide in higher education: the UFC and the PCFC are clearly separated. The universities will, thus, continue to receive more money for a student than the colleges and polytechnics, even though that student is studying for an identical qualification. Differential funding will lead to differential quality of provision and the stratification of institutions in terms of status and esteem. Without subventions to compensate for this and to enable them to make their own particular innovations, and without a vigorous relationship with their LEAs, polytechnics and colleges may find themselves increasingly becoming second-rate universities. On the other hand, some commentators have seen the Act as moving towards an eventual unitary system of higher education. Commenting on the consultation papers the CDP pointed to the benefits that would accrue if the two funding bodies adopted the same approach to procedures and performance measures: it would then be 'possible to obtain comparable data and to use comparable measures when assessing the cost efficiency of institutions' (quoted in Haviland, 1988, p.252). The CDP were obviously confident that the results of such comparisons could only show the relative cost-effectiveness of their institutions. They might anticipate that such data would prepare the case for a shift towards more parity in funding levels across the binary divide.

This sanguine view overlooks the trend towards greater and more overt stratification within the university sector itself via the introduction of research rankings. The danger for polytechnics and colleges is that courses recognized as receiving inferior funding will be offered to a different type of student, whose ultimate qualifications may also come to be recognized as inferior. The Act may solidify rather than erode the binary divide within higher education. In continuing differential funding, now under the same central control, the Act both disadvantages the polytechnics and misses the opportunity to move universities in the direction of courses sufficiently flexible to meet a wider range of student needs and interests.

The consultation documents issued by the DES before publication of the Bill (DES, 1987a,b) indicated not only the tightness of the Secretary of State's grip on the two funding councils but that, further, a completely new approach to funding might be adopted. In particular the documents proposed that the funding bodies would 'tender' to the institutions, with the implication that they would then compete on a cost basis as to which would receive the student allocations: who can provide the leanest and fittest BSc in Engineering? Who can train the cheapest doctor? The actual arrangements of the Act, particularly following its amendment, are considerably more restrained than the documents that preceded it. Nevertheless, the Secretary of State now has considerable central control via the two funding councils.

Fears about how this power may be used have been voiced in particular by the university sector. In responding to the consultation round J.R. Quayle, Vice-Chancellor of Bath University, stressed the inappropriateness of the new powers to be given to the Secretary of State in a 'non-totalitarian civilized country' (quoted in Haviland, 1988, p.236). Totalitarian use of the new powers remains unlikely: what is less certain is whether or not they will be used to enforce competitive tendering. What is certain is that the government is determined that higher education should be more actively involved in engendering and propagating the so-called culture of enterprise.

At the end of 1987 the Department of Trade and Industry (DTI) launched, via the MSC, its first foray into higher education. In terms of an offer of up to one million pounds per institution, the universities, colleges and polytechnics were invited to participate in the 'Enterprise in Higher Education' programme. The scheme is 'designed to encourage the development of qualities of enterprise among those seeking higher education qualifications' (MSC, 1987, p.3). This initiative is not intended to be a bolt-on for a few students on a few courses, but is rather to be 'integrated into the education provision of the institution with the aim of providing opportunities for all students within an agreed timetable' (MSC, 1987, p.4). Irrespective of higher education's own aims for students, and, in some cases, potentially in opposition or at least irrelevant to them, the Training Commission has placed the culture of enterprise on the undergraduate agenda.

The point here is not concerning the appropriateness or otherwise of this initiative: it is rather that central government is prepared to involve itself in the actual definition of the content of higher education courses. At first this was via the MSC carrot of additional funding, but now that the Act is passed the government has at its disposal the much more powerful DES stick. Furthermore, this initiative was a pure example of the government's own predominant ideology (see Chapter 2). While it must be emphasized that totalitarianism remains a long way away, this initiative with its clear ideological intentions (there was no money available for courses on, say, collective action or individual freedom) may be seen as political interference in higher education. It remains to be seen whether the 1988 Act is used by the government to travel further down this road: it certainly gives them the ability to do so.

The new funding arrangements and the notion of tendering will bring enterprise into higher education in another way. Given the priorities of efficiency and cost-effectiveness, the assumption must be that the government intends higher education institutions to compete for students and funds. Enterprise is to be both the process and the content of higher education. But, as with other sectors of education provision, behind the rhetoric of competition is the fact of much greater central government control.

Neither state control nor the enterprise culture need in themselves be pernicious to higher education. The issue is the extent to which institutions will remain free to develop autonomous skills and knowledge. Such development is only irrelevant to the needs of the national economy where those needs, and indeed that economy, are too narrowly and unimaginatively defined.

REFERENCES

* Committee of Enquiry into the Academic Validation of Degrees in Public Sector Higher Education (1985) *Academic Validation in Public Sector Higher Education*. London: HMSO.
* Committee of Vice-Chancellors and Principals (1985) *Report of the Steering Committee for Efficiency Studies in Universities*. London: CVCP.
* DES (1987a) *Changes in Structure and National Planning for Higher Education: Contracts between the Funding Bodies and Higher Education Institutions*. London: DES.
* DES (1987b) *Changes in Structure and National Planning for Higher Education: Polytechnics and Colleges Sector*. London: DES.
* Haviland, J. (ed.) (1988) *Take Care Mr Baker! The Advice on Education Reform Which the Government Collected But Withheld*. London: Fourth Estate.
* MSC (1987) *Enterprise in Higher Education*. London: DTI.
* Scott, P. (1988) Higher education. In Morris, M. & Griggs, C. (eds), *Education – the Wasted Years? 1973–1986*. Lewes: Falmer.
* Simon, B. (1988) *Bending the Rules: The Baker 'Reform' of Education*. London: Lawrence & Wishart.
* Young, H. (1987) Demoralised dons in search of a champion. *Guardian*, 10 December p.21.

8
The Ideological Contradictions of Educational Reform

David Coulby

This chapter details six contradictions concerning the 1988 Education Reform Act. These are either: within the Act itself; between elements of the Act and the government's other educational policies; or between the Act and wider areas of government policy. The contradictions are related to the ideologies, here frequently referred to as rhetorics, that have preceded and surrounded the legislation. In conclusion the contradictions within the ideology from which the Act emanated are considered in more general terms.

The next chapter deals with another sequence of policy contradictions which are seen as being structural. The distinction between structural and ideological contradictions is purely operational. The two categories are by no means mutually exclusive: there are both structural aspects to the ideological contradictions and ideological aspects to the structural contradictions.

Contradiction here implies the ways in which one aspect of policy tends to negate another. However, the term also implies a further meaning, that of conflict and in particular class conflict. The policy contradictions identified here are often related to wider aspects of class conflict and the way in which state policy attempts to participate in such conflict. Similarly, although ideology can, in an everyday sense, imply simply rhetoric, it may also be used to denote a system of beliefs predicated upon the class position of those who uphold and propagate them. The ideologies used to legitimate the Act and those that it seeks to propagate are ultimately related to the class interest of its exponents. The ideological contradictions of the Act, then, can be related to wider conflicts of production and reproduction. The treatment here looks mainly at the self-negating aspects of ideological contradiction, but the wider implications are not forgotten and are returned to in the final section.

110

CONTRADICTION 1: VOCATIONALISM AND TRADITIONAL KNOWLEDGE

Up to the passing of the 1988 Act there had been a common claim that schools had played a part in the economic decline of the UK. As mentioned in Chapter 1, Margaret Thatcher's buccaneering speech to the 1987 Conservative Party conference provides a *locus classicus*:

> We want education to be part of the answer to Britain's problems, not part of the cause. To compete successfully in tomorrow's world—against Japan, Germany and the United States—we need well-educated, well-trained, creative young people. If education is backward today, national performance will be backward tomorrow.

> (Thatcher, 1987)

As was outlined in Chapter 1, this rhetoric proposed that schools, and particularly secondary schools, were filling the minds of young people with dissident notions and counter-establishment propaganda. The familiar bestiary included peace studies, anti-racism and anti-sexism.

The wider fear of sociology and social science enquiry fuelled the concern. There were many areas of the secondary school curriculum where such enquiry could be encouraged, ranging from economics and business studies, through active tutorial, to home economics. Every one of these subjects is excluded from foundation subject status in the national curriculum. The secondary and, for that matter, the primary and potentially the tertiary curricula are neutered of all controversial or possibly dissident modes of enquiry. Of course, some foundation subjects, particularly English but also history or even science, are able to include critical or social analyses. In this respect, it will be interesting to see if the Secretary of State uses his control over the programmes of study to ensure that in these curriculum areas potentially critical topics are eschewed.

The traditionalist nature of the national curriculum may well betray the atavistic predilections of those who cobbled it together, but it also represents the safety embodied in useless knowledge. If young people can be returned to reciting the capes and bays of England there is, as far as the upholders of this position are concerned, less time for them to be dabbling with potentially, or even explicitly, dangerous notions, such as the gender division of labour.

The contradiction here is with vocationalism which, within the rhetoric of the same government spokespersons, had previously been presented as the educational panacea. Chapter 1 indicated the way in which the government and its agencies in the early 1980s attempted to blame the dramatic rise in youth unemployment not on structural economic change, nor on their own economic policies, but on the schools and the young people themselves. The rapid rise of the MSC (as it then was) as an agency for training the post-16 age group was presented as the remedy. The MSC, with the tacit support of the DES, even succeeded in penetrating the curriculum of the compulsory years, via the TVEI coup. TVEI brought the message of vocationalism to secondary school students.

Although it was initially viewed by some teachers and authorities with suspicion, TVEI has proved to be an interesting development in secondary schools (see Chapter 5 for a discussion of some of its surprising results). The deliberately differential funding of the TVEI resulted in some areas, schools and pupils receiving provision lavishly superior to that available to others. A variety of different developments occurred within the scheme but standards of technical and employment-related education were achieved in many places that served to allay the suspicions based on previous MSC interventions. The results of TVEI were far from exclusively narrow and vocationalist. Those LEAs which had initially stood back did eventually seek to become involved.

Technology is to be a foundation subject but the Act contains no reference to vocational education within the curriculum. The previous vocationalist rhetoric appears to have been abandoned. The two ideologies of standards and vocationalism had long stood uneasily together. In opting for the former, in the reified version of traditionalist knowledge, the Act offers little protection to those developments made in the name of the latter.

The contradiction between vocationalism and traditional knowledge is a function of the stratified secondary curriculum. What this stratification actually offers is standards for a few (the Prime Minister's inflexibility in the face of any proposals to change A-levels is relevant here) and vocationalism for the rest. The contradiction here is at the deeper level suggested in the preamble to this chapter: it is an aspect of the conflict between mental and manual labour, which is based on the mode of production. In this sense the preference shown for traditional knowledge in the Act seems less surprising. It is possible to predict with some confidence that vocationalism will find its way into the national curriculum of some students. The Act in its wider intentions is designed to extend and reinforce social hierarchy not to eliminate it (see contradiction 3 below).

CONTRADICTION 2: FREEDOM AND CONTROL

The rhetoric legitimating the proliferation of different forms of schooling is that of freedom of choice. This is one of the over-arching ideologies of the new right. Local financial management, centrally funded schools and city technology colleges are seen as widening parental choice. The assisted places scheme had pre-viously been justified as a way of giving parents the opportunity to escape from the LEA monopoly and increase their consumer choice. Repeated flirtations with the voucher scheme indicated the seriousness with which the ideology of choice in education was to be addressed. Inextricably linked to the notion of choice is that of competition: if choice is increased, schools will need to compete more effectively to recruit pupils (or to recruit a certain kind of pupil) and this competition will improve the standards of all concerned. As described in Chapter 2, the infallibility of the market is seen as a mechanism for improving the education system.

These rhetorics are now justifying an attack on comprehensive schooling and possibly on state education as such. The prolifer-ation of forms of schools is designed to reinstate a differentiated and structurally stratified system. Parents—those, that is, with cars or able to afford the transport—will be able to choose schools in more distant areas where perceived standards are higher. Voluntary-aided schools will be able to be more open in their application of admissions criteria. Parents will be free to prefer all-white schools to those where there is a racial mix. The idea of the common school for all was never effectively operationalized in the UK: the principle is now totally overthrown. CTCs will assist in the break-up of the comprehensive system and join with private schools in attempting to attract the more academic pupils away from local schools. Competition certainly will increase and the ideology of competitiveness will be further legitimated. Schools in less privileged areas will see their pupil numbers dwindle as more privileged parents airlift their children out to CTCs or to opted-out schools. The slum school is about to be recreated. It will be the province of the local authority sector, which will then doubtless be vulnerable to further attacks on account of poor standards.

The contradiction is not between the ideology and the structural changes. The rhetoric of freedom has long been used to justify privilege in terms of the maintenance and support of the fee-paying school sector. The contradiction is actually between two components of the Act: while freedom is the justification for choice and differentiation at a structural level, freedom at the curricular level is to be dramatically restricted. The right-wing Institute of

Economic Affairs has emphasized the way in which the national curriculum broke the sacred tenet of the market:

> The most effective national curriculum is that set by the market, by the consumers of the education service. This will be far more responsive to children's needs and society's demands than any centrally imposed curriculum, no matter how well meant. Attempts by Government and by Parliament to impose a curriculum, no matter how 'generally agreed' they think it to be, are a poor second best in terms of quality, flexibility and responsiveness to needs than allowing the market to decide and setting the system free to respond to the overwhelming demand for higher standards. The Government must trust market forces rather than some committee of the great and good.
>
> (quoted in Haviland, 1988, p.28)

The Institute can be seen to have spotted this contradiction. Parents are to be free to choose a school for their children but not free to choose what is taught there, which is the exclusive territory of the Secretary of State. Except for those in the privileged sectors of fee-paying schools and CTCs, freedom of choice over curriculum matters is to be dramatically curtailed for schools, teachers, parents and pupils. The proffered freedom of choice is illusory: parents are free to choose which institution will slavishly teach the Secretary of State's curriculum to their children. Far from extending freedom the 1988 Act is a shift towards epistemological totalitarianism.

The rhetoric of competition is frequently linked with that of freedom. Competition is portrayed as a radical and libertarian philosophy which will return power to the consumers and break the education 'monopoly' of LEAs. In generating competition between pupils, teachers and schools, the Education Reform Act, it is claimed, will shake up the complacency of schools and teachers and thereby lead to a general raising of standards.

In fact the Act is more likely to lead to the reinforcement and reproduction of patterns of social division in terms of class and race. Educational institutions are part of the mediating process whereby patterns of social stratification are reinforced or eroded: they are far from determinants of social division. The main forces behind the patterning of social stratification are economic. To the extent that educational institutions play a part in this process, the Act, with its licence for competitiveness, will lead not to greater freedom and opportunity but to greater stratification. This developing stratification will be firstly along the lines of class, with richer families having access to CTCs and opted-out schools via the familiar mechanisms of admissions tests and/or superior mobility. Racial stratification in schools is also likely to increase. Many white parents are likely to embrace enthusiastically the opportunity to remove their children from schools where there are significant black populations. Whether the emergence of educational segregation will help or hinder the opportunities of black people remains to be seen, but it is difficult to see how such segregation can encourage the emergence of a racially equal society.

CONTRADICTION 3: LOCAL AND CENTRAL CONTROL

Perhaps the easiest contradiction to expose is that of local autonomy, invoked to defend local financial management and opting out. It is not only parental freedom that the centralist powers of the Act diminishes, it is also the framework of local democratic control. Just as the curriculum has been brought under central state control, so educational decision-making has been shifted from local authorities to central government. The formidable list of new powers taken on by the Secretary of State for Education and Science has led to bitter protests from both major political parties (see Chapter 1).

There are sound arguments that both the substance and the organization of education should be under democratic local control to allow the maximum responsiveness to local conditions, choice and needs. When education is linked to local government there is a requirement that those with responsibility for schools should have a mandate from the electorate. In the arrangements of the Act, representation on the governing bodies of schools, colleges and polytechnics is dramatically and explicitly removed from local authorities. Instead a large number of governors, at all levels, is to be drawn from the world of industry and commerce and from the professions. As well as having no electoral mandate, these people are drawn exclusively from one side of the world of work: there is no requirement, for instance, that there should be trade union or trade council representation on governing bodies. The people selected to be governors are likely to be predominantly of one political persuasion: the same as that of the party which introduced the Act.

If the control of education had just been removed from local authorities to the central state, there would still be an argument that this reduced democracy rather than enhancing it, since it shifted important decisions away from more responsive and accessible (and no less democratic) authorities. In fact the Act does give considerably more powers to the Secretary of State, but it also removed democratic participation in governing bodies while at the same time enhancing their powers over those of elected local government. By means of the new governing bodies and non-democratic bodies, such as the NCC and SEAC, the Act ensures that even those decisions not taken centrally are awarded to people likely to have the same political leanings as the (Conservative) central government.

The arrangements on opting out (see Chapter 3), despite the double ballot device still allow 1 per cent of parents with pupils at a school to determine that a school should opt out of its local authority. This travesty of a democratic process is justified in the rhetoric of local control and parent-power. The government's response to the ILEA ballot is illuminating with regard to its true attitude to parental and local views. While the Bill was still before Parliament, a ballot was carried out among all parents of school-age children in the ILEA. An absolute majority of all parents was clearly against the break up of the authority. The results of this ballot were disregarded by the government.

The Act is not designed to give control to local participants such as parents or governors. It is designed to take control from LEAs. It is from them that control of the schools, colleges, polytechnics and the curriculum is to be withdrawn. The rhetoric of parent-power masks the politics of centralization. The rhetoric of local control masks the withdrawal of important educational decisions from the democratic process.

CONTRADICTION 4: NATIONALISM AND INTERNATIONALISM

A surprising component of the national curriculum is the requirement that all secondary pupils should study one modern foreign language for five years. The important question is which modern foreign language or languages the schools will be instructed to study. The opportunity exists for the national curriculum to recognize and enhance the linguistic diversity of the UK. Languages such as Bengali, Punjabi, Turkish and Greek are widespread in this country, especially in urban areas. Curricula and appropriate exam syllabuses have already been developed in some schools to make the languages of at least some of the communities of the UK available at secondary level.

The ideology behind the Act, however, is such that it is unlikely to be used to develop community language teaching. At primary level, in the wake of *The Swann Report*, the government is actively discouraging the teaching of community languages and the development of bilingual skills. The Act is painstakingly free of any reference to multiculturalism or anti-racism. Its terms of reference and aspiration are not those of a pluralist society but of competitiveness within the frame of a narrowly conceived nationalism. It is likely then that modern foreign languages will be conceived in the academicist framework evident elsewhere in the national curriculum. The programmes of study are yet to emerge, but it is likely that the modern foreign language in the overwhelming majority of schools will be French.

The case of Welsh highlights the lack of acceptance of other forms of linguistic diversity. Welsh is to be compulsory in Welsh-speaking areas at primary level and across the Principality at secondary level. There is even to be a special quango for the Welsh curriculum. The Act, by contrast, completely fails to recognize the existence of any other minority language. The black communities of the UK are apparently not seen as language groups.

The contradictions that emerge from this concern the privileging of academicism as against practicality and vocational relevance. If the community languages were more widely and vigorously taught then that would, in the first place, allow the people of the UK to communicate better with one another. Many more opportunities for practical bilingual interaction exist actually within many schools, particularly those in urban areas, than can be derived from an annual outing to Calais. Furthermore, although France is certainly a major trading partner, the predilection for this particular modern foreign language can hardly be justified on commercial or vocational grounds. The community languages of the UK include major international languages spoken by large segments of the world's population, such as Spanish, Bengali, Chinese and Portuguese. French no longer provides access to commercial, scientific or diplomatic contact of this magnitude. To stress modern foreign languages without reference to the actual linguistic diversity of the UK is demonstrative of a Eurocentric notion of knowledge and culture that is in contradiction to the insistence on the role that educational institutions should play in strengthening the position of the nation in the international marketplace.

The failure to escape narrow nationalism and to address the international composition of the nation's population and culture may well hinder developments in other areas of the national curriculum. It will be interesting to see the extent to which the programmes of study address multiculturalism and internationalism. *The Kingman Report* (DES, 1988) on the teaching of English confirms fears that ethnocentric versions of knowledge are to be revived. It is encouraging that these versions have not been adopted, so far, by the Working Group of the NCC.

CONTRADICTION 5: SPECIAL EDUCATIONAL NEEDS AND NATIONAL NEEDS

With regard to children perceived to have special educational needs, the contradiction is between two pieces of educational legislation introduced by Thatcher administrations. An examination of this contradiction exposes what are likely to be some of the most profoundly damaging effects of the Act. The 1981 Education Act legislated, although in far from the strongest terms, for the integration of pupils perceived to have special needs into mainstream schools. This Act gave LEAs several pretexts, including cost, for not implementing the integration policy. Indeed, in the seven years between the two acts, progress on integration was slow. Different authorities adopted contrasting policies and so there were wide variations in the percentages of children statemented and of those attending segregated special provision. Authorities such as Oxfordshire continued to eschew segregation and others such as the ILEA, Somerset and Newham adopted vigorously integrationist policies. A start had been made in tackling structural and attitudinal difficulties. The goal of integration was gradually becoming more widely accepted among teachers in both mainstream and special schools.

The 1988 Act largely ignores pupils perceived as having special educational needs. They are almost totally absent from its specifications. Some flexibility with regard to the delivery of the national curriculum to such children is offered. This is a derisory acknowledgment of those profoundly challenged children and young people who are hardly likely ever to make more than a start on the core and foundation subjects.

Even among those children whose perceived learning and/or behaviour difficulties do not fit into clinical categories, there will be many for whom the obstacle course of the national curriculum, with its four assessment points, will be little more than a parade of failure, frustration and stigmatizingly proclaimed humiliation. The TGAT-style testing arrangements (see Chapter 4) will ensure that such children are labelled early, labelled often and labelled with the full force of school, local and national norm-referencing. To claim that the effects of this labelling on their motivation will be such as to raise standards is to engage in cynicism.

While the curriculum and testing sections of the Act are likely to be harmful to pupils perceived to have special needs, the structural sections actually reverse what limited progress was made under the 1981 Act. If there is to be competition between schools in a locality, then this will be largely on the basis of the results of the four-stage assessment. Children with learning and/or behaviour difficulties are precisely those likely to reduce a school's 'average', thereby making it less attractive to parents. The other important criteria in competition, those that compose fragile local reputations based upon student demeanour, sports results and a well disciplined, academic ethos, are unlikely to be boosted by the presence of pupils perceived to have special needs. Head teachers and governors who have to compete will be increasingly unwilling to admit such pupils. CTCs and opted-out schools will find ways of excluding them, particularly those perceived as having learning and/or behaviour difficulties.

Financial delegation may prove another pressure against integration. It is doubtful that the funding mechanisms will be sufficiently sensitive to ensure that resources are delivered to those children with special needs in mainstream schools. Resourcing has always been included in the argument of those who wish to drag their feet over the implementation of integration. Local financial management may provide them with the argument that the only effective way to deliver adequate resources to pupils perceived to have special needs is through the mechanism of segregated special schools.

The pressure over competition, combined with uncertainty over resource allocation, will lead head teachers and governors of mainstream schools to seek to increase rather than reduce the segregated provision. The demand will be to take such pupils back into special schools and units so as not to damage the competitive edge of the under-resourced mainstream schools. Those schools, possibly grant-maintained or CTCs, that manage to ensure that there is a minimal number of pupils perceived to have special needs among their intake may actually be seen as the most successful. The rump LEA schools, transformed by free parental choice into born-again slum schools, will be the ones with the least power to resist (or indeed, since it is wrong to assume that integrity need be lost in the competitive market, with the least inclination to resist) a disproportionate number of pupils perceived to have special needs among their admissions.

As outlined earlier in this chapter, structural stratification of schools will develop as a result of parental choice. Those pupils with learning and/or behaviour difficulties will be concentrated with other working-class children in schools with the lowest amount of parent appeal and probably with the lowest level of resources. The 1988 Act will more than reverse the limited

119

progress made under the 1981 Act. The pupils likely to be the most adversely affected by its implementation are those perceived to have special needs, particularly those with learning and/or behaviour difficulties.

CONTRADICTION 6: POPULIST CAPITALISM AND STATE POWER

The contradictions surrounding the Act are related to wider fractures within the populist capitalism of which it is but one manifestation. Successive Thatcher governments have attempted to assist the restructuring of international capital in the UK. Large profit rises and huge tax cuts for the richest section of society are indicative of substantial success in this respect. However, in this process the administrations have become increasingly intolerant of any source of oppositional or alternative views. The metropolitan counties and the ILEA have been eliminated. The BBC is under perpetual scrutiny and attack. The higher educational institutions have been brought under much closer central state control. The contradiction is between the rhetoric of populist capitalism and the reinforcement of state power.

One aspect of the populist rhetoric is that of revived nationalism. Crystallized in the conflict with Argentina, British (or perhaps English) nationalism is also invoked to support economic competition. Its less welcome manifestations include the violent jingoism of English football supporters. Racism remains an important aspect of this nationalism. The anti-anti-racism perpetrated by the 1988 Act (see Chapter 3) is one aspect of this. Continued British support for South Africa is another. Post-imperial English nationalism provides familiar distractions and scapegoats in an era of high unemployment and working-class defeat and impoverishment.

It is the rhetoric of freedom, however, that has been most centrally adopted by populist capitalism. This rhetoric is used to conceal the practice of privilege and the radical redistribution of wealth and power away from the working-class. Free to buy their own council houses, shares in British Telecom and membership of BUPA, the British working-class have suffered a substantial reduction in their collective bargaining power and a rapid decline in their national health provision. They are free to send their children to fee-paying schools, free to opt out of their trade unions and free to participate in the febrile privatization programme. These freedoms are contradictory. They are actually manifestations of the enhanced power of those whose interests are antagonistic to the working-class. Freedom to purchase private schooling is actually the legitimating rhetoric for those privileged classes who seek to reproduce their position through educational processes. Freedom to withdraw from trade unions only assists capital's endeavours to reformulate its dominance. Freedom to participate in the purchase of the nation's public assets merely provides derisory substantiation for the ideology that the poorest strata participate in the wealth of the richest. Those with a few shares in the privatized industries are reluctant to support their unions or any opposition lest their meagre gains are taken from them. Meanwhile, via regressive taxation and cuts in the public services, the progress of decades has been reversed.

The schools, colleges, polytechnics and universities had become potential platforms for dissident views. Apparently autonomous from both the state and its capitalist base, they had, in a small way, developed possibilities for the development of critical and oppositional modes of enquiry. The 1988 Act brings them under the tighter control of the central state. It is not, in this respect, contradictory to the interests of state power seeking to assist the reformulation of capital. It is contradictory to the interests of the working-class who have been the victims of the ideology of populist capitalism.

REFERENCES

- DES (1988) *Report of the Committee of Enquiry into the Teaching of English Language* London: DES.
- Haviland, J. (ed.) (1988) *Take Care Mr Baker! The Advice on Education Reform Which the Government Collected But Withheld.* London: Fourth Estate.
- Thatcher, M. (1987) Speech to the Conservative Party Conference.

9
Structural Contradictions

Leslie Bash

CONTEXT

Having examined some of the major ideological contradictions arising from the 1988 Education Act the analysis now moves to the area of structure. What is important here is the frequent lack of coherence in the institutional sphere and the contradictions and conflicts at the level of social action. In order to be able to undertake this analysis it is necessary to restate certain points concerning the general ideological struggle that has been waged at the level of the central state over the past 15 years.

As was argued in Chapter 2, ideologically the primacy of the market has now been firmly established and, as a result, the political culture has undergone a significant transformation. The prevailing ideology is to accept the view that social stability depends upon the individual pursuit of economic gain; its attainment contributing to an enriched nation ready to take its place among the most powerful in the world. The allocation of resources cannot be controlled by the state; a productive economy cannot result from centralized planning. In short, it is now asserted that government has no part to play in manufacture or, increasingly, in the provision of services. Privatization and consumer sovereignty walk hand in hand as the twin ideological components of Conservatism in the 1980s.

At first sight, the 1988 Education Act is the epitome of this market philosophy. As we have pointed out in earlier chapters, the Act allegedly seeks to move the control of education away from those considered to be the producers (teachers and local authority bureaucrats) and to the consumers (parents and employers). Essentially, such control is not to be seen in political terms (apart from increased parent and employer representation on governing bodies). Rather, parents and employers will increasingly be in a position to effect change in the way schools, colleges, polytechnics and universities operate, through their actions as consumers of

122

educational services. Thus, the predicted outcome must be that the education system delivers what the customer demands.

This poses an ideological dilemma of some significance. The economic liberalism espoused by the current Conservative administration lies somewhat uneasily with demands for a more coordinated system of education and training designed to meet the challenge of foreign competition (see Chapter 2). Whether this is a legacy of a bygone age of European national pride—a kind of latter-day Disraeli or Bismarckian conservatism—or merely a demand for greater coherence is neither here nor there. What is at issue is the conflict between the necessity to plan and a policy based on the free play of market forces. This, it can be argued, is one of the major difficulties facing capitalism today. While the market and consumer sovereignty remain ideologically strong, the reality of increased concentration of production and the necessity to see competition in international terms has meant that long-term planning is vital to the future of industry. While cabinet ministers accept that the market should decide the outcome of take-overs of British-owned industries they might also note that the behaviour of hungry foreign-based multinationals is frequently the consequence of long-term planning and of support given by their own governments.

The surprising thing is not that competition, enterprise and other ideological categories should have been taken on board so readily by the Conservative government of the 1980s but that any notion of planning by the state should have been so easily thrown out. Indeed, in terms of education, this does not accord with what has happened: the past decade saw the ascendancy of the Manpower Services Commission and, as a consequence of the 1988 Act, a whole new machinery (UFC, PCFC, NCC and SEAR), together with the extension of powers to the Education Secretary, has legitimized centralized educational planning.

Most of all, the imposition of the national curriculum gives the lie to the prominence of libertarian conservatism. Indeed, it is this that has caused considerable unease on the right of the political spectrum. Where is the freedom of the individual to pursue his or her own ends when the central state acts in an undeniably collectivist manner? It is not surprising that organizations such as the Institute of Economic Affairs, for long the provider of ideological support for contemporary Conservatism, have expressed disquiet at the current direction of educational policy. Nor should there be amazement that representatives of the establishment in the Church of England dare to accuse central government of totalitarian tendencies.

CONTRADICTIONS IN A DIVIDED SOCIETY

Contradiction is a helpful term for it can denote different things. In structural terms, two distinct uses may be discerned, the first corresponding to the inconsistencies and illogicalities within the structures themselves and the second denoting potential or actual conflict between collectivities. Ideologically, the central state has attempted to present Britain as a unified society and yet the glaring ideological contradictions outlined in the previous chapter have their corollary in a fractured nation.

The ideological contradictions in the educational debate are thus manifestations of deeper structural conflicts. It is of little use to pretend that culturally and structurally Britain constitutes a homogeneous entity. Not only is British society riven by deep divisions of class, race and gender, it is also characterized by a state apparatus that is frequently at odds with the demands of capital, despite the supposed identity of interests. This might be seen as the consequence of uneven historical development within the ruling class: feudal remnants dying alongside the rise of multi-national capitalism and computerized money markets. Alternatively, the thesis of relative autonomy suggests that the different institutional structures within the capitalist state develop their own momentum and do not necessarily conform to the logic of the system. (For further development of these arguments see Poulantzas (1978), especially Part 4.) Likewise, within the population as a whole conventional patterns of living rooted in taken-for-granted modes of behaviour conflict with the apparent need to change, to be flexible, to be rational. Following this, a number of important structural contradictions need to be examined within the context of the 1988 Education Act.

CONSUMER CHOICE VERSUS RESIDENTIAL PRIVILEGE

The first structural contradiction lies in the apparent significance of the consumer in education. Although education continues to be defined largely in terms of schooling, the patterns of its consumption will tend to be constrained by the practicalities of access to schools. In other words, residential patterns are crucial to patterns of educational consumption. Both schools and houses tend to be spatially fixed, a fact that is frequently overlooked by those who advocate a market approach to the provision of these commodities.

On the other hand, the spatially fixed nature of schooling and housing can be exploited by those parents who have the economic power to manipulate the supply of both. The more affluent families will often move to a locality because of access to a particular school and, in so doing, will contribute to the reproduction of class relations as manifested in space. This, of course, complicates matters when it comes to collective action on the part of parents, producing contradictions at the micro-level. While middle-class parents, when resident in downtown areas, may struggle for better schooling in association with working-class and ethnic minority parents, their allegiances are bound to alter when they decide to take flight.

Even if they remain in the maintained education sector, the middle-class can use economic power to move to better housing in more desirable localities, and thus make nonsense of the optimistic view that people will unite across the class divide to protect collectively provided services (see Castells, 1977, 1983). This view depends very much upon the ability to distinguish one sector of provision from another, each with a particular mode of access. Thus, although people may inhabit different housing or labour markets, they may, for example, send their children to the same schools. Often this is no more than a passing fancy, representing a romantic attachment by some of the wealthier parents to an egalitarian ethos.

Residential privilege extends beyond the simplistic middle-class–working-class divide. The extension of home ownership through council house sales has affected working-class families, but it has not always resulted in the extension of material wealth in practical terms. Home ownership does result in a 'cache of resources stored in privately owned housing' leading to greater accessibility to private sector services (Lowe, 1986, p.79) or at least to the possibility of moving to where there are alternative public sector services.

It is likely that in an era of open enrolment, popular schools will tend, more than ever, to be situated in middle-class suburban areas. Likewise, unpopular schools are likely to coincide geographically with unpopular residential districts, notwithstanding the recent gentrification of inner city areas (such as London's Docklands). It may be that the influx of young, middle-class, relatively wealthy families will result in changes for the better as far as the local schools are concerned (increased popularity with a greater social mix, injection of funds, more stable well qualified teaching staff). On the other hand, it may make little difference if the new residents constitute households with two large incomes and no children or if they send their children to fee-paying schools.

In short, existing social divisions, manifested in spatial segregation, are likely to be reinforced as a consequence of the 1988 Act. In particular, the difficulties facing urban schools are exacerbated as the more politically and economically powerful parents exercise their choice, with the polarization between the more favoured localities and the poorer inner city areas becoming even more marked. Within a capitalist economic framework the operation of the market ostensibly allows for *individual* freedom of action— forgetting that individual actions are shaped and circumscribed by collective experience and structural constraints.

Within the urban context such individual freedom amounts to little more than privilege for the affluent. They do have the choice of whether to live in the countryside, the conventional residential districts of cities or some new development area like the Isle of Dogs. Since the long-term operation of the capitalist system signi- ficantly shapes patterns of work and residence it is clear that freedom of choice is something of a chimera. It is therefore difficult to imagine that a single-parent family on Income Support living in a run-down urban tower block will have the same choice regarding the children's schooling as the two-income professional family residing in a semi-detached in a leafy suburb. More poignantly, the Nottinghamshire Education Committee asks:

> In a system based on market forces, what choices are avail- able to those who are neither socially mobile nor academi- cally able? The committee considers that one consequence will be an emigration to the more favoured suburbs from the inner-city areas for those who are both mobile and academi- cally able, leaving those who are already disadvantaged in other ways with no choice but to attend a school which may not even be in their area.... The overall effect is divisive, expensive and educationally unsound.
>
> (quoted in Haviland, 1988, p.171)

Before we leave the urban context, it is worth noting the obvious policy contradiction involved in the breaking up of the ILEA. The ILEA, as a Labour education authority, was a target for the loony left campaign waged before the 1987 general election. However, many of the boroughs to which control of education is now to be given—Hackney, Lambeth, Lewisham—are precisely those that in their other policy initiatives have been much more severely castigated than the ILEA. Control of schools and colleges has been taken away from a left-wing authority to be given to left-wing authorities! Moreover, these authorities will have to place educa- tion within the context of other priorities, such as housing, refuse collection and road repairs, which because of rate capping and a general fiscal crisis may lead to the very opposite of what was intended by the 1988 Act. An impoverished borough like Hackney, already characterized by tremendous difficulties in the delivery of adequate education, could well experience a lowering of standards rather than the raised ones envisaged by the Secretary of State.

CONSUMER CHOICE VERSUS EDUCATIONAL EFFICIENCY

The structural contradictions of the 1988 Act are most clearly seen in the urban context but they will be keenly felt in the nation as a whole. Here, the conflict between the promotion of parental choice of school and the expressed need to run education in a business-like manner becomes apparent. Many observers have already concluded that educational institutions are coming to resemble manufacturing and retail enterprises and that the new legislation merely hastens this process. It has been noted that schools and further and higher educational institutions are increasingly subjected to industrial organizational and accounting procedures. These often reflect the latest fashions in management technique, in which head teachers, school governors, college principals and others must be initiated (no doubt leading to an even greater proliferation of relevant courses). Consequently, there is some degree of irony in a situation where British manufacturing industry continues to decline as a result of the inertia of management and the failure to invest, while the education system is purportedly being set on the road to greater efficiency and responsiveness to demand.

By all accounts the maintained school system still remains largely unmoved by this quest for greater efficiency. Local authorities are blamed for allowing schools to operate at a less than efficient level, while the DES frequently prevaricates over, or even prevents, the closure of those that might be viewed as uneconomic. This is surely the message transmitted by the Audit Commission when it reported that:

> Over 1,800 [secondary] schools were well below the guideline of a minimum of ... 900 pupils. The situation is likely to get worse over the next few years unless the current rate of about 50 closures a year is increased to over 100.

> (quoted in *The Guardian*, 4 August 1988)

The question is how consumer choice is to be maintained in the wake of an efficiency drive. The Secretary of State has already hinted that opting out of LEA control will not necessarily save a school from closure or amalgamation if plans were already in progress. Nevertheless, one of the attractions being offered to head teachers by those attempting to encourage them to bid for grant-maintained status is that they would thus be free from local authority interference. It is spelt out clearly that such interference involves, among other things, closures and amalgamations. There are those within the government who are likely to want schools to opt out at any price. Thus the facility for schools to opt out is likely to hinder the efficient use of resources as the Audit Commission sees it. LEAs will be hindered in their rationalization programmes because any school threatened with closure or amalgamation will be able to make the counter-threat of opting out. The Act will actually lead to inefficient planning and resourcing of schools. It is a tricky contradiction that central government will increasingly have to face—and attempt to resolve—as it grapples with the conflicting beliefs in choice and efficiency.

SOCIAL COHESION VERSUS THE OPERATION OF THE MARKET

In broad perspective, the 1988 Education Act is significant as part of a general trend towards the depoliticization of public life. Much of this has been documented by Habermas (1976) and more recently by Bauman, who has pithily remarked that Thatcherism:

> offers the public a massive programme of *buying oneself out*, singly or severally, from politics; of making politics irrelevant to the pursuit of individual or collective goals and ideas. . . . What makes such presentation credible is the parallel reduction of political power to the role of a purely constraining force, and an emphatic surrender of its *enabling* function.
>
> (Bauman, 1988, p.37)

Accordingly, it substitutes the market and individual action for planning and collective decision-making, leaving only issues of social control as worthy of consideration by the state. The irony is that as the former gains ground so the latter comes increasingly to the fore. Given the legitimacy of the market and competition the likelihood of deviant means being adopted to achieve accepted goals is increased. The temptation is to concentrate on those involved in the informal economy, so-called social security scroungers, and street crime. What is frequently ignored by the state guardians of morality is the blurring of boundaries between the activities of stockbrokers, certain investment fund managers and fraudulent financiers. The money-making culture has far more significance for those who already possess substantial economic power!

The widening gap between the wealthiest and the poorest, between those in employment and those who are not, may be testimony to the failure of post-war social and economic policy—

not least that aspect concerned with educational reform. For it was conventional wisdom in the 1950s and 1960s that the democratization of education and the creation of what became known as equality of opportunity would result in a more harmonious, less divided society. That it has not appeared to have done so is a pointer to the fallacy of such a simplistic ideology. The backlash of the 1970s and 1980s has perhaps exposed some covert but none the less fundamental aspects of the national culture, especially in relation to the desirability of equality as a social objective. In other words, hierarchy, whether in terms of class, race, gender or perceived ability, may be a deeply embedded cultural norm in the UK.

Governments have to live with the consequences of their ideologies and actions. Social divisions are acceptable, even laudable, if there is a good deal of public consent, e.g. that the unemployed accept the collapse of work, that ethnic minorities become resigned to institutionalized racism and that women perceive limits to their full participation in economic and political life. Unfortunately, most people who are unemployed actually want to be in work. Apart from the acceptance of the Protestant ethic and the feeling of social solidarity arising from being at work, there are remunerative advantages when compared with the dole! Likewise, members of ethnic minorities are less and less tolerant of racism and put up resistance in a variety of ways. Finally, despite the persistent obstacles placed in the way of women, there is a continuation of the struggle for equality. The difficulty for the central state thus arises when people, as a consequence of rising expectations, do not play the game.

SOCIAL CONTROL VERSUS CORPORATE FREEDOM

The final structural contradiction relates to one of the fundamental aspects of current government policy: the maintenance of social control. Except in the government's overt insistence on a tougher approach to issues of law and order, and its emphasis upon the renaissance of the family as the custodian of traditional values, such policy often remains below the surface. Its stance, however, tends to emerge in other ways, particularly in the guise of sympathetic attitudes towards the plight of those who are disadvantaged, especially in the inner cities.

Evidently, the government has been disturbed by the manifestations of the distorted spatial social structures that characterize the large metropolitan areas. Indeed, the inner cities became an important symbolic aspect of the Conservative Party's 1987 general election campaign. Money has not been spared in public relations efforts to arouse awareness of threats to the social fabric together with the means to combat them. Hence the emphasis upon drug abuse, AIDS, garden festivals, etc. Even here there is a limitation on involvement by the state. Social control is one thing; social provision clearly another.

It is against the backcloth of government disengagement from welfare that its support for private development and sponsorship should be judged, especially in relation to inner city infrastructural policy. The central role of private enterprise in the London Docklands has its parallel in the move to establish city technology colleges: both allegedly function as catalysts to hasten economic development and, thus, to provide employment and a higher standard of living for all. On reflection a somewhat different picture emerges. Private industry is not in the business of philanthropy; it is in business on its own account—indeed, it has to be, for this is fundamental to the operation of the capitalist system. Paramount is an overriding duty to the shareholders to maintain and, if possible, to increase profits. In the UK industry has, on the whole, sought to do this without seeing a parallel duty to the public at large to provide civil amenities, public housing, etc. (with a few exceptions such as the Quaker firms of Cadbury and Rowntree), or a duty to provide education and training for its employees, let alone the nation's children.

Consequently, the redevelopment of the Docklands area provides high cost housing for the City dealers and PR executives while easing out the local inhabitants, ignoring both their accommodation and their employment needs. Likewise, city technology colleges, if sponsored by industry, must provide something in return (for example, a refusal to sanction anti-smoking propaganda in the case of the CTC to be established with financial support from British American Tobacco). Despite rhetoric to the contrary, the establishment of CTCs and the erection of riverside residences on the Isle of Dogs are essentially divisive in their consequences, with the contradictions clear for everyone to see. Private housing compounds exist cheek by jowl with council high-rise accommodation while CTCs will provide schooling for a potential elite. Meanwhile, the other schools in the locality compete, in a market distorted by the presence of the CTC, for customers and funds in order to operate the national curriculum effectively.

The central question of the essential function of education dominates any consideration of structural contradictions. It is difficult to evade the proposition that for the majority of the population schools are experienced as mechanisms for social control. Whether they are effective as such is neither here nor there; what is important is that teachers, parents, police and others in authority over young people see schools in this way. If one result of the Act is the reinforcement of social divisions, the perpetuation of alternative structures characterized by sub- or counter-cultures will remain unchecked. This may well lead to the further proposition that those in support of the free-market ideology but who also wish to maintain a traditional hierarchy of social relations have never really had much time for universal education. The 1988 Act seemingly incorporates both the free market and the social hierarchy yet still perpetuates the desirability of universal education, based on a uniform curriculum, at least until the age of 16. This has not been without its critics on the right of the Conservative Party (such as Rhodes Boyson), who have questioned the assumption that children need 11 years of compulsory schooling.

If the market replaces social control as the basis for the existence of viable educational structures the consequence may be, in the long run, the establishment of alternative means of dealing with those young people who reject (or who are rejected by) conventional schooling. Ostensibly, CTCs are to be set up to provide the country with a highly skilled technologically oriented labour force. However, given that the idea has not drawn in the industrial sponsorship that it was intended to, the cynical view that CTCs will essentially be there to perform an ideological function has been reinforced.

There is now an additional proposal to establish modified CTCs (CTCAs), which will specialize in arts technology, film and video with the hope that they might attract young people from inner city ethnic minorities. Leaving aside the implicit racism contained in this innovatory move, it is revealing as an ideological mechanism. To put it another way, here is a policy that states: it is possible to demonstrate that not only is Britain in the forefront of technological education for young people, it is also tuned in to their interests and, furthermore, it has found a way of contributing to peace in the inner cities.

Surely the 1988 Education Act, whatever the intentions of the Secretary of State may have been, is now revealed in its consequences and in the context of previous social and educational policy as a major tool of social control. In the midst of the establishment of a uniform national curriculum there has begun the process of re-establishing the institutional segregation that existed before the moves towards comprehensivization, multiculturalism and integration of pupils with special needs.

In the years that follow this Act parents will have to accommodate their choice to the consequences of selection—whether overt or hidden. Employers, while paying lip-service to industrial training taking note of profiling and records of achievement, and demanding flexibility on the part of recruits, will make use of the segregated educational system to sort out the sheep from the goats. Teachers—and, more importantly, pupils and students—will be caught in the middle. The extent to which they will be able to make sense of it all depends on whether those involved in practice in schools, colleges, polytechnics and universities can draw up a new, authentic educational agenda. The final chapter makes some tentative comments in this direction.

REFERENCES

Bauman, Z. (1988) Britain's exit from politics. *New Statesman & Society*, 29 July.

Castells, M. (1977) *The Urban Question*. London: Edward Arnold.

Castells, M. (1983) *The City and the Grassroots*. London: Edward Arnold.

Habermas, J. (1976) *Legitimation Crisis*. London: Heinemann.

Haviland, J. (ed.) (1988) *Take Care, Mr Baker! The Advice on Education Reform Which the Government Collected But Withheld*. London: Fourth Estate.

Lowe, S. (1986) *Urban Social Movements*. London: Macmillan.

Poulantzas, N. (1978) *Political Power and Social Classes*. London: Verso.

10
Postscript: Towards a Fresh Agenda

Leslie Bash

This is the point at which the critical observer is in danger of either writing a conclusion so beset with platitudes that it was not worth the effort, or else calling the people to the barricades to overturn a bankrupt political regime and herald in the new Jerusalem. It is important therefore to examine the possibilities not only of salvaging whatever appears to be of benefit from the 1988 Act but also of a fresh approach to educational policy and practice. Above all, it should signal the abandonment of the agenda set by Prime Ministers Callaghan and Thatcher and by Secretaries Joseph and Baker. The new agenda must be predicated upon the slaughter of some sacred cows while reasserting fundamental tenets of educational progress and democracy.

To enable consideration of the basis for a new educational agenda there is a need for a brief assessment of the Act. From the previous two chapters, in which numerous inconsistencies and conflicts were highlighted, the only sensible conclusion about the 1988 Education Reform Act that can be drawn is that it is a ragbag of measures. The one thing that it is not is a coherently planned, carefully considered piece of legislation. Therefore, it is not surprising that some aspects of the Act might be viewed as progressive by those who see themselves in the radical or socialist tradition in education. The establishment of a national curriculum and apparently greater autonomy for the polytechnics and higher education colleges are not necessarily reactionary moves; the increased participation of parents in the governance of schools is not in itself a bad idea.

The construction of a new agenda must, first of all, involve some questioning of the nature of the educational process itself. It is not relevant to rehearse the old arguments concerning the aims of education; it is a tedious activity, only serving to present intending teachers with thinly disguised ideological positions. As a social institution, education must be assumed to be structurally linked with other institutions: the state, the economy, the family, religion, the arts and so on. It is of little help to protest about the incursion of politics, work, the demands of parents or popular culture into schools. It is quite clear that schooling is a worldly pursuit and the sooner this is recognized by all those involved the better. However confused and socially divisive the 1988 Act is, at least there is no pretence that education should remain untouched by those on the outside.

The task must be to establish authentic links between educational institutions and the outside world while at the same time retaining a critical perspective. Pupils in schools as well as students in further and higher education should be aware that education is not simply concerned with the achievements of narrowly defined extrinsic goals—obtaining employment, induction into a specific religious creed, or fulfilling the hopes and desires of parents—but neither is it insulated from them. What the Act does, therefore, is raise contentious issues regarding the nature of education, issues that have frequently been avoided or ignored by teachers, local education authorities and teacher-educators.

The first of these issues is that of the national curriculum. That the curriculum should continue to be the preserve of individual teachers is an assumption to be challenged by those who argue for educational democracy. Certainly, the establishment of a national curriculum with ultimate control by the Secretary of State is of profound political significance. But while, on the one hand, it appears to centralize and straitjacket educational practice and to make it vulnerable to whichever ideology happens to be dominant at any one time, it does, on the other hand, carry with it elements of democracy. This is not in the sense of freedom or autonomy, but of equalization. Indeed, there is nothing inherently progressive about teacher control of the curriculum, nor is there anything democratic about variability in curriculum delivery. At least in principle, parents, children and teachers can now expect a certain degree of consistency in curriculum delivery between schools throughout the country. If schools are to be characterized by a greater uniformity in curricular matters one consequence may be closer co-operation between teachers and between parents.

This last point is crucial for the re-establishment of education as a political concern. The authors have suggested that one of the successes of the Thatcher government has been to depoliticize much of what has hitherto been part of the public realm. This has been brought about ideologically, mainly through the careful exploitation of the mass media, by asserting that society is largely a fiction and that only individuals (and their families) matter, particularly in their role as consumers. This ideology has its counterpart in the treatment of workers as individual producers, each responsible for her or his own success or failure. The 1988 Education Act appears to reinforce such ideology but, paradoxically, teachers and parents could emerge with a far stronger collective voice than they have had before.

Take the case of the teachers. There is a forceful argument which states that the quest for professional status has frequently cut teachers off from the concerns of parents. Professionalism has often meant a tendency to treat parents as ignorant of educational matters, even in the case of their own children. Trade unionism among teachers, while combining the struggle to raise salary levels and conditions of service with a general concern for the improvement of education, has often prevented the emergence of a political and communal awareness. By this is not meant the need to ally with a political party; rather, the importance of making links with parents at the school level and with other sections of the local community.

Teachers may also now be in a position to achieve a greater degree of unity at the national level. The label of 'profession' has always had something of a hollow ring about it when applied to teaching: not only are teachers fundamentally divided by type of institution, level of qualification, skills and knowledge demanded and rewards given, they have also hardly achieved the kind of occupational control expected of professionals. Perhaps the 1988 Act will inject some new life into teachers as a collective association. Centralization of educational control, as with the rise of the factory system of manufacture in the nineteenth century, may encourage the formation of a new collective consciousness among those who work in schools, FE colleges and institutions of higher education. It is hoped that this will be in alliance with those who stand to benefit from a better education system: in the first place parents, who have a genuine interest in the well-being and future of their children; secondly the providers of employment, who correctly recognize the raising of the educational level of the nation as vital to its survival; and finally, and most importantly, the pupils and students themselves.

The second major issue is that of the governance of educational institutions. In so far as changes in the control of schools and colleges and the abolition of the Inner London Education Authority have been perceived as part of the attack on local government they have been experienced at best as acts of cynicism and at worst as acts of vandalism and destruction. Yet these changes may place power in the hands of those deemed to be even more radical than the displaced and partially disenfranchised local authorities. It is highly unlikely that 100 per cent of schools able to opt out of LEA control will do so, thus leaving the new London authorities with time to work out and implement their education policies. The key to the success of such policies will be in the ability of LEAs to gain the confidence of parents, employers, and other local interest groups. The ILEA's London Compact, for example, has shown an innovative approach towards the school–work transition that could be emulated by other authorities. Ironically, the abolition of the ILEA could result in a good deal of experience and expertise in this and other progressive policy areas being sent to LEAs throughout the country as well as to the inner London boroughs.

As far as the opted out schools are concerned, teachers will be brought face-to-face with having to deal directly with the DES and with the loss of LEA support. That this may challenge some of the assumptions of teachers is a good thing. The sections of the Act dealing with further and public sector higher education may also prompt teachers to reflect on the fact that new demands will be made upon them—in addition to the increased demands of the past 10 years. In effect, if FE and HE lecturers now have to behave as members of business organizations, they may well look to the world of business as their reference point—and demand comparable remuneration and working conditions.

On the other hand, the Act may in practice have little immediate effect upon educational practice for the vast majority of educational institutions. This is the view contemplated in the leader column of the *Times Higher Education Supplement* on the day the Act received the Royal Assent (29 July 1988). But since the conclusion of that editorial is that the Act is 'designed for political effect rather than educational advantage' and that it is 'not much about education at all. Rather it is an attempt to impose on schools a theory of society', then it might be concluded that its consequences are likely to be political rather than educational. That, however, does not mean that there will be no changes to the education system: the authors have attempted to demonstrate that some aspects are to be fundamentally altered.

The point is that it is possible for the forces of educational democracy and progressivism to take the initiative. It is to be hoped that this will not be in the form of the creation of embattled enclaves of radical practice, as in the 1960s and 1970s (although it may come to this), nor in publishing theoretical studies for academic reflection (necessary though these are), but rather in involvement in local and institutional policy formulation.

Name Index

137

Subject Index

Subject Index

Primary schools—*cont.*
  and the national curriculum 63–4, 65
  and opting out 39
Principals, college 80
Racial inequality and racism 89, 90–1, 92–3, 95–6, 120, 129
Racial segregation 34–5, 50, 97, 115
Rathbone Society 67, 68
Religious education 3, 56, 61
Residential privilege 124–7
Robbins Report (1963) 4
Schools Council, abolition of 9
Secondary schools
  curriculum 6
  and financial delegation 35
  and the national curriculum 56, 64–5
  and opting out 39
Secretary of State for Education
  and city technology colleges 41
  and grant-maintained schools 40
  and higher education 103, 104, 106, 107–8
  and the national curriculum 56–7, 59–60, 65, 67, 69
  and the new London LEAs 94
  and planned admission levels 32
  powers under Education Reform Act 3, 20, 27, 115–16, 123
Sexism and sexual inequality 12–13, 15, 89–90
Social control 129–32
Social sciences 61–2, 111
Social Security regulations, and young people 73, 83
Special educational needs 37, 46–8, 118–20
  and YTS 76, 83
Special schools 35, 56
Swann Report 116–17
Teachers 132, 135, 136
  and the curriculum 3, 6, 54–5
  erosion of professionalism 9–10
  and financial delegation 37–8
  and the ILEA 97
  and the LCC 87
  and the national curriculum 65, 69

strikes and pay dispute 9–10, 14, 17, 93
trade unions 3, 37, 44–6, 51, 97, 135
university 102–3, 104–5
Technology teaching in schools 62, 64, 65, 112
Tertiary colleges 74, 82
Testing, and the national curriculum 57, 66–9, 118–19
TGAT (Task Group on Assessment and Testing) 57, 64, 65, 66–7, 68, 69, 70, 118
Tower Hamlets 92–3, 95–6, 97
Trade unions 29, 115, 120, 121
  and financial delegation 37, 38
  and grant-maintained schools 41
  and the MSC 8
  teachers 3, 44–6, 51, 97, 135
Training (formerly Manpower Services) Commission 8, 73, 78, 79, 80–1, 82, 108, 123
TVEI (Technical and Vocational Education Initiative) 8, 36, 62, 77–8, 79, 80, 112
Tyndale affair 88, 89
Unemployment 3, 7–9, 63, 72, 79, 112, 129
United States 85
Universities 3, 81, 100–1, 102–3, 104–5, 107, 108
  and the free market 25
University Funding Council (UFC) 104, 107
University Grants Committee (UGC) 101, 102, 104
Vocational preparation courses 76, 77
Vocationalism 74, 75, 79, 82–3, 111–12
Voluntary schools 27, 35, 41, 94, 113
Voucher system 27–8, 113
Welsh language teaching 56, 90, 91, 117
Working class
  and freedom 120–1, 125, 126
  and further education 74–5
  and higher education 5
Youth, control of 72–84
Youth Training Scheme (YTS) 8, 26–7, 72, 75–6, 79, 80, 81, 83